Julian Assange had a cold
his voice was hoarse
and two octaves
lower than usual
even so
on this particular day
he didn't speak
as softly
as he usually does
sometimes
he speaks so softly
it makes you think
you're going crazy
you cling
to his every word
utterly concentrated
and still only
understand
half of what he's saying
and begin wondering
if you've got a hearing problem
and ask yourself
if he's doing it intentionally
in this exceptional situation
so that maybe
no directional microphone
can filter
what he's saying
so on this Monday
at the end of October 2013
Julian Assange
had a cold
and a hoarse voice
he was wearing
faded jeans
and a Veterans for Peace
blue hoodie
and a black baseball cap of the
Sea Shepherd Conservation Society

16-01-2013 12:38 pm — At the post office. Queuing up.

that hunts down
the hunters of
whales
and seals
and dolphins

On this particular
morning
Assange's breakfast
started out with
a generous gulp of
Glenfiddich Single Malt
twelve years old
he cleared his throat
after the first sip
his voice sounded
fuller
less hoarse
he took
a second sip
"Whiskey"
he said
"is the best remedy
for a cold"
and outside
in front of the window
there was a London police officer
and Assange smiled
and said
"Okay so now
let's arm
this thing"

"The thing"
a parcel with
a mobile inside
modified
so that it shoots
a picture every 10 seconds

16-01-2013 12:42 pm — At the post office. I'm next.

through a small hole
in the cardboard
and transmits
the picture live
to the Internet
at the same 10 second interval
the mobile's GPS
uploads
the location of the parcel
then there are six batteries
connected
to the mobile's battery
to ensure weeks
of transmitting time

"The idea began"
says Carmen
"with a pizza"
in Ecuador
in August 2012
the foreign secretary proceeded
to announce whether
Julian Assange
would be given asylum
or not
Assange
accused in Sweden
of sexual harassment
by two women
had fled
from an international
arrest warrant
to the Ecuadorian Embassy
in London
dressed
as a mailman
so they say
to escape possible extradition
to the United States

16-01-2013 12:44 pm — Postal worker at post office puts parcel in postbag. Parcel is on its way.

where allegedly there is
a secret indictment
against him
the contents of which
are not even known
to his lawyers
and numerous US politicians
reportedly declared
that because of his role
as the founder of WikiLeaks
it would be best
to have him shot
without trial
and in London
police surrounded
the Embassy
and threatened
to storm the building
TV-teams were ceaselessly
uploading their
filmed footage
to the internet
causing an international
uproar

Along with Doma
her husband
and artistic partner
Carmen kept track
of what
was happening
in their studio in Zurich
the two of them
are the core
of !Mediengruppe Bitnik
they watched on
"Reuters TV"
"Russia Today"
"Guardian"

16-01-2013 12:44 pm — Parcel is inside postbag. Parcel with running camera is on its way to Julian Assange.

Twitter
collected information
in a variety of chats
for example on 4Chan
a forum
that offers anonymity
4Chan they say
is the cradle of the collective
Anonymous
and in this forum
hundreds of users
followed what
was happening in London
on live streams
"What can we do for Julian?"
somebody asked
at some point
"They must be hungry
cordoned off
in the Embassy"
somebody else wrote
"I guess I'll order a pizza
for them"

A few minutes later
Doma and Carmen
and everybody else
keeping track of events
on whatever channel
saw a man on a motorbike
from Domino's Pizza Service
approach the house
wondering why
there were so many
policemen standing around
and pushing his way
through the officers
to ring the bell of the Embassy
and speak

16-01-2013 3:32 pm — Bag being picked up. Where to next? Meanwhile have informed Julian Assange about parcel.

to a security officer
who apparently tried to explain
of course you couldn't hear it
that no one here
had ordered a pizza
and shortly thereafter
another delivery man
appeared
and then another
complete confusion
world wide coverage
police officers
Assange
WikiLeaks
international
diplomatic crisis
and pizza from Domino's

And then
on 16 August 2012
Ecuador's Foreign Minister
Ricardo Patiño
declared
also live on air
that Julian Assange
could not expect to get
a fair trial
in the United States
and that he should therefore
be given asylum
Ecuador
a small country
population 14 million
facing down a world power
in South America
you can win
an election
with symbols like that
and in front of the Embassy

16-01-2013 3:57 pm — Total blackout since 3:33 pm. First doubts arise. Maybe someone taped camera?
16-01-2013 4:08 pm — Still black. But we have just checked Geoposition and packet is moving!
16-01-2013 4:27 pm — Still black, but packet is now near Haggerston Park, East London.
16-01-2013 5:24 pm — Parcel is moving. Hackney Central. East London. Image black. Camera broken?
16-01-2013 5:34 pm — Parcel moved to East London Mail Centre, Whitechapel, London.

in London
WikiLeaks' supporters
broke into cheers

"What can we do next?"
a user asked on 4Chan
"A taxi"
another wrote
"Julian needs a taxi
to take him to the airport
so that he can fly from there
to Ecuador"
and shortly afterwards
dozens of taxis
and black limousines
drove up
to the Embassy in London
with "Mr. Assange" signs
in the windshield
and traffic broke down
in the narrow streets
in front of the Embassy

"It was a fabulous five hours"
Doma says
"on the one hand
it was a live experience"
Carmen says
"You sit at the computer
and have no idea
what's next
because at some place or another
kids are sitting at the computer
thinking of ways
to interfere
in what's happening"
Doma says
"On the other hand"
Carmen says

16-01-2013 7:28 pm — Parcel arrived at Mount Pleasant Post Office. This is main central London post office. Parcel still in bag.

"the taxis
the limousines
that were waiting for Assange
who had just been given asylum
but couldn't take
a single step
outside
the Embassy
were making
a political statement
and besides
sending taxis
live on all the channels
is an extremely
personal intervention
into the midst
of a geopolitical event
suddenly
hanging around on 4Chan
having watched
developments
from ordering pizza
to the appearance of
the delivery vans
we felt as if
altogether
we had confronted
abstract geopolitics
with our personal history"

"During Occupy Wall Street
for example" Carmen says
"people painted signs
to say why they
were part of the 99 percent
the student with huge debts
the man who can't live on his pension
who probably didn't have
much in common

16-01-2013 8:30 pm — Suddenly view of Central Post Office.

but because of
a personal issue
were now united
in the protest
of the 99 percent"

That's what inspired
the idea of sending
Julian Assange
a parcel
one with a manipulated mobile
so that like usually with
live transmissions
anybody on the net
could trace
its path
curated and with comments
by !Mediengruppe Bitnik
on their own Twitter account
almost in real time
a live ticker
from a post office
in Hackney
all the way to the
Ecuadorian Embassy
Flat 3B 3 Hans Crescent
just behind
the luxury
shopping centre
Harrods

The Man from Guatemala

Doma spent three weeks
building the parcel
customizing the mobile
testing the batteries
the live transmission
through a go-between

16-01-2013 8:32 pm — Central Office Assembly Line.

Mike of The Yes Men
a group of activists
Doma and Carmen
made contact with people
closely associated
with Assange
"Our only concern
was to make sure
he knew
he'd be receiving something"
Carmen says
"We didn't want
the Embassy
or Assange
to feel threatened
because when scanned
the parcel
with the mobile
and the wiring
and the batteries
could be mistaken
for a bomb"

In the message
they sent
Assange
Carmen and Doma
wrote
"When you receive
the packet
could you please
1. Show us
your view
of the diplomatic crisis
unfolding
outside the Embassy
2. Send the camera on
to a person
of your choice"

16-01-2013 8:33 pm — View from the trolley.

Early January
via a contact person
an activist from Guatemala
a terse message
arrived
through the network Tor
where nothing and no one
leaves traces behind
"Julian agrees"
nothing more
nothing less

"We didn't know
how Julian would react"
Doma says
"We didn't even know
if the parcel would get that far
I flew from Zurich to London
built three identical parcels
in Adnan's flat
two of them
were replacements
in case the first
got intercepted
Adnan
also belongs to Bitnik
for the past ten years
he's been recording our work on film
hundreds of hours of footage
no idea
what we're going to do with it
so I set up
an encrypted video chat channel
in Adnan's kitchen
with Carmen in Zurich
and
with our son Leano
if he wasn't
at the day care centre

16-01-2013 8:45 pm — A person. Parcel is still at Mount Pleasant Post Office.

or sleeping
the channel was always open
kitchen to kitchen
three whole days"

After a first
sleepless night
Doma sent off the parcel
at an Indian newsagent's
in Hackney
on the way to the post office
he fixed
one last bug
in the software
at the last moment
he had noticed
that the mobile
would crash
and switch off
after a thousand photographs
but in the end
there were over ten thousand pictures
on the first picture
at 12:38 pm
you see Doma
taking a picture of himself
with the parcel
in the mirror at the newsagent's
at 12:44 pm the parcel disappeared
in a red mail pouch
and from there
the camera transmitted
darkness
for hours

The minute the parcel had been sent
Carmen started tweeting
on the account set up
specifically for this happening

16-01-2013 8:58 pm — Person walking away. Person pushing trolley.

number of followers
at that point
zero
the first tweet
at 12:30 pm 16 January 2013
read
"Sending Julian Assange a parcel
containing a camera
camera documents its journey
through postal system in realtime
#Assange"

The first retweets came in straightaway
"And soon afterwards
our server was
overrun" Carmen says
"our computer
wasn't getting one hundred inquiries
a minute anymore
it was getting 30,000
it was about to crash"
"For the next couple of hours
I had no idea what
was happening
in the outside world"
Doma says
"I didn't leave the flat
for two days
I was in this film
nonstop
for 36 hours
two whole nights
constantly worrying
that our system would crash
that something would go wrong
at the same time
we were telling the story
of the journey on twitter
organizing extra servers

16-01-2013 8:59 pm — Parcel is being moved. View of the hall.

because ours was overloaded
and kept sending
error messages
and talking to journalists
I felt like
a pressure cooker
about to explode"

"@bitnk hi there
Dave from the tech desk
at BBC news here
are you happy for us
to use the pics?"
"Vice"
"La Stampa"
"Ars Technica"
"Huffington Post"
Globo
"El Comercio"
"Nation of Swine"
Swiss Radio
"And Julian Assange's
mother
expressed her enthusiasm
on twitter"
Doma says

"We were overwhelmed"
Carmen says
"we didn't know
if anyone
besides us
would even notice the whole thing
or think
it was interesting"

On twitter
and Internet forums
people started

16-01-2013 9:07 pm — Judging from this image, parcel must be in a bag. Green this time.

debating
on the platform
"Hacker News" for example
someone wrote
"definitely think
this is a bad idea
if Royal Mail
finds out
they might destroy
the parcel"
someone replied
"And that's a bad thing?
I don't think
they're concerned
about property damage
they're doing it
to see
what happens"

At a Snail's Pace to the Embassy

At 5:16 pm
the parcel stopped
sending signals
the screen went black
and Doma panicked
"Dammit all
is that it?"
After staring
in despair
at a black screen
for an hour
Doma suddenly thought
he'd noticed
a change
"Didn't the black
just change colour
a little bit?"
he asked Adnan

16-01-2013 10:34 pm — Totally dark. But packets Geolocations are changing. Now on Kings Cross Rd.
16-01-2013 10:35 pm — Packet is moving fast. Now on Grays Inn Rd.
16-01-2013 10:37 pm — Black. Now at Kings Cross Station.
16-01-2013 10:43 pm — Image is still black. Moving down Euston Rd. towards Regent's Park.
16-01-2013 10:48 pm — On Edgware Rd.
16-01-2013 10:50 pm — On A40 now. Really moving fast.
16-01-2013 10:53 pm — Still black. Parcel inside van. On A40 near East Acton Station.
16-01-2013 10:56 pm — A40 near North Acton Station.
16-01-2013 10:59 pm — A 40. Western Avenue, Ealing.
16-01-2013 11:04 pm — Hangar Ln. Now Gunnersbury Av.
16-01-2013 11:08 pm — Great West Rd. Now Hogarth Ln.
16-01-2013 11:12 pm — Great Chertsey Rd, Hounslow.
16-01-2013 11:18 pm — Twickenham Rd, Richmond.
16-01-2013 11:25 pm — Hampton Rd E, Feltham.
16-01-2013 11:29 pm — Godfrey Way, Hounslow.
16-01-2013 11:33 pm — Arrived at Ceva Logistics, Godfrey Way, Feltham.

"isn't it more of a
light black now?"

Signal and movement
at 6:01 pm
from East London
to a distribution centre
in the city
Mount Pleasant Mail Centre
the mobile
had probably been
in a dead spot
the Embassy was coming closer
but now there was so much
traffic
that the server crashed
Doma and Carmen
had just managed
to get it up and running again
to manage network traffic
by setting up several servers
when the camera started
sending pictures again
the first picture from
the Royal Mail system
a brightly lit sorting office
in Whitechapel
men loading parcels
pushing trolleys back and forth
at 9:07 pm the parcel
was transferred to a green mail pouch
before
continuing its journey
around midnight
but not
in the direction of the Embassy
instead in a completely different one
out of the city
out of London

17-01-2013 12:42 am — Outside the bag again.

"Why? Why? Why?"
Doma screamed and
smoked five cigarettes
and Adnan
so immersed in the action
that he'd forgotten to give
his students
a seminar couple of hours earlier
brewed him
a relaxing cup of tea
Carmen
online via video chat
was convinced
that the parcel
wherever it was
was going to be destroyed
it moved 22 kilometres
towards Heathrow
where it stayed
and the screen went black again
around 2:30 am in the morning
a foot briefly came into view
but then
the parcel was not blown up
instead
at 5:32 am
early in the morning
it was driven back
to the centre of town
to another sorting office
very close to the Embassy
"Why take a parcel
with a downtown destination
out to Heathrow first
and then back again?"
somebody asked on Twitter
another follower tweeted
"The #royalmail route optimisation process
could use some work!"

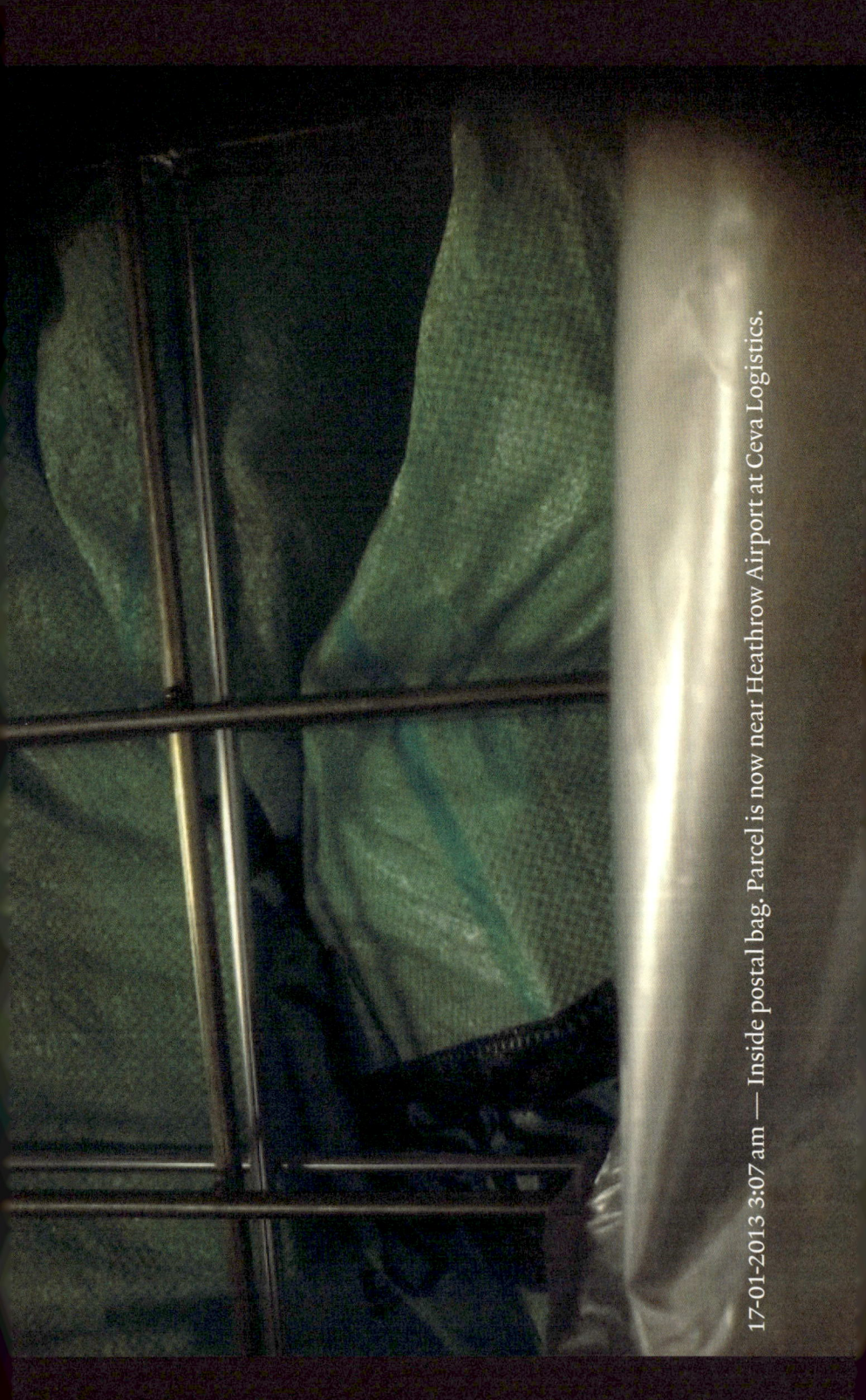

17-01-2013 3:07 am — Inside postal bag. Parcel is now near Heathrow Airport at Ceva Logistics.

"What I have learned
from @bitnk
parcels spend
a great deal of time
in total darkness"

After another
sleepless night
Doma saw
that the parcel
had started moving again
on 17 January
at 10:34 am
the GPS signal wandered
in the direction of the Embassy
but then
practically there
only a few hundred metres left
its progress
was excruciatingly
slow
advancing at a snail's pace
for two hours
it was practically
within touching distance
of the Embassy
without getting there
"@bitnk
might it be
that the postman
is following you
and has a fine sense
of suspense?"

Through the pictures
now transmitted by camera
you could tell
that the parcel was actually
in a postal

17-01-2013 3:10am — All dark. Once again.

delivery van
a door
opening and closing
the interior of a van
full of parcels
the piles diminishing
until at some point
you could see it in the pictures
there was practically only
this one parcel left
and when
after two hours
the parcel still hadn't been
delivered
viewers in front of their screens
gradually began
getting restless.

"Hey Bitnik
when will this parcel
be delivered?
I really need to get
some work done"
"Hurry up Bitnik
No one is working at our office
Parcel already
ruined my morning"
"I've been watching this
for 24 hours
I'm exhausted"
"I just spent
the whole day
watching a parcel
making its way
to Ecuador
It's been
fucking fascinating
and I don't really know
why"

17-01-2013 6:06 am — New View. Out of bag.

"this is more exciting
than the mars rover"
and Marina Galperina
from "Animal New York"
blogged with a time delay
"What is the meaning
of this
parcel blitzkrieg?
What else
is in this
mysterious parcel?
Why can't I stop gawking
at the crotch-level interiors
of some foreign post office?
Why are these Twitter updates
so addictive?"

Then the postman
took his lunch break

To Doma and Carmen
totally exhausted
as they were
the minutes
seemed like hours
deliverance
came an hour later
at 2:04 pm
after 25 hours on adrenaline
and it came
as a tweet
from @wikileaks
"Live camera
posted through mail system
to Assange
with GPS tracker
now streaming
from postal van
outside Embassy"

17-01-2013 8:27 am — Maybe this is still a postbag we are looking at.
17-01-2013 8:32 am — Mostly dark again. But things are moving.
17-01-2013 8:34 am — Light seems to be flashing. Image changes from dark to this alternating every 10 seconds.
17-01-2013 8:36 am — Even more light now. But image is blurred. Is parcel in a bag again?
17-01-2013 8:38 am — Dark again. We are still near Battersea Park Railway Station in London.
17-01-2013 8:53 am — There are still flashes of light sometimes. But mostly image is dark.
17-01-2013 9:29 am — Still in Vauxhall, Wilcox Rd. Image still dark. Maybe parcel is in a van?

"So then we knew"
Carmen says
"that they'd noticed
and were playing along
by which time
I was so nervous
I felt like I was having
to give a speech
to 15,000 people
and in a way
we did give a speech
to 15,000 people"
Doma replied
"@wikileaks
can
you
see
the
van?"
@wikileaks replied
"will the MI5 open it?"
half an hour later
at 2:49 pm
@wikileaks wrote
"@bitnk
package has arrived
and is now
with Embassy security"

Great rejoicing
in Adnan's and in Carmen's kitchen
and on Twitter too
only one former London postman
complained by e-mail
that he had
worked
at the security scanner
in one of the sorting offices
through which the parcel

17-01-2013 9:49 am — Parcel still at Royal Mail Jubilee Mail Centre. Waiting to be delivered to Assange.

had passed
for 10 years
and would never
absolutely never have
allowed that parcel
through

"Welcome to Ecuador"

Then delivery was delayed
one hour
two hours
three
in the meantime
on Twitter
hundreds of users
were writing down
what Doma and Carmen
were hoping
or fearing
they envisioned
every single possibility

"I'm quite sure
they will blow it away
because it looks strange"
and "There is definitely
still a good chance
that we will see
Julian Assange's
smiling facc"
and "Initiate mass hysteria"
and "Perhaps you should have
put something nice to eat inside"
and "The last 50 feet
always takes the longest"
and above all
"Don't want the battery
to die now"

17-01-2013 9:50am — View of a chair.

"Later Julian told us"
Carmen says
"the parcel
actually did
provoke a minor crisis
the then ambassador
thought there would be
trouble of some kind or other
if photographs
from inside the Embassy
were leaked to the outside
or she was just worried
about the hullabaloo in general
and she wanted
the Foreign Minister himself
to release the parcel
not until Assange
had made it clear to her
that the BBC
was reporting live on the proceedings
did the ambassador
give her go-ahead"

At 6:19 pm
the head of
a mountain lion
suddenly
came into view
or a bomb-sniffing dog?
Then a carpet?
A leather couch?
One journalist wrote
"I've been to the Embassy
I recognize the couch"
and the official twitterer
of "Huffington Post"
lost his cool
"Julian give us a wave!
Julian Julian give us a wave!"

17-01-2013 9:51 am — Some people standing around, are they discussing the contents of the parcel? #assange #mailart

A card with writing
appeared in the picture
"Is this thing on?"
then another one
"Hello world"
and then
Julian Assange
appeared
in the picture
in a WikiLeaks sweater
he smiled
and held up
more cards
in front of the camera

"Welcome to Ecuador"
"Free Bradley Manning"
"Free Nabeel Rajab"
"Free Anakata"
"Free Jeremy Hammond"
"Free Rudolf Elmer"
"Free Anons"
"Justice for Aaron Swartz"
"Transparency for the state!
Privacy for the rest of us!"
"Postal art is contagious"
"Thank you Ecuador"
"Thank you to all supporters"
"Keep fighting"
"2013 we win!"
"Fin!"
"Out of cards!"

The picture
turned black again
as it had done countless times
in the hours before
when we weren't sure
if the parcel

had ended up in a rubbish bin
or at MI5
"Because at least
since WikiLeaks
issued a statement on twitter
all the secret services
in the world
knew about this art happening"
as Carmen says
an event that
transported
Julian Assange
stuck in a flat in London
essentially unfiltered into the flats
of thousands of viewers
so that you almost had
the feeling
you'd met him personally

@WeRAllAnonymous tweeted
"many thanks
to !Mediengruppe Bitnik artists
for some of the best entertainment
I've ever had on Twitter
We salute thee!"
Christine Assange
Julian's mother
wrote
"it's wonderful
to see Julian smiling
& happily enjoying the moment
#Assange Embassy
package-cam
from @bitnk
just showed us
artistic creativity
has extraordinary
political power"
and somebody tweeted

17-01-2013 9:59 am — Good view of the space. Nice Image.

"yeah
@bitnk definitely won
the Internet
today"

Then Doma tweeted
"back to black"
when Assange
disappeared
after his performance
and the screen turned
black again
at 7:31 pm London time
on 17 January 2013
at the end of the by now
32-hour live transmission
Carmen tweeted
for the thousands of viewers
who had followed
the events live
on the Bitnik website
and on Twitter
she tweeted
as if everything
had gone according to plan
as if the Assange performance
was to be taken for granted
"This was
a LIVE Mail Art Piece by
!Mediengruppe Bitnik
featuring Julian Assange
Thanks and goodbye!"
and in Adnan's kitchen
in Hackney
when the adrenaline
had worn off
Doma slowly
collapsed
after two sleepless nights

17-01-2013 10:07 am — In the trolley, waiting for inspection.

"In an age of total
digital surveillance
in which every e-mail
is read by NSA"
says Doma
"we wanted
to take advantage of
the good old policy of
postal service secrecy
still operative in Europe
to see
what would happen
if we sent Julian Assange
a parcel
nowadays a letter
is safer than e-mail
e-mail
from Switzerland to England
can now be read
by various countries
it's not as easy
with a parcel
because of postal secrecy
parcels and letters
can't simply be opened
but we still wondered
if it would actually be delivered
Or frisked?
Or detonated?
Or bugged?
Scanned by the secret service?
Make an alarm go off?
Would it get through the barriers
that separate
Assange from the outside world?
We had in fact
reckoned with different images
with someone from security
opening the parcel

17-01-2013 10:29 am	—	Black. Parcel must be in bag or box again.
17-01-2013 10:34 am	—	Moving again. Fast. Now on Hartington Rd.
17-01-2013 10:37 am	—	Parcel has just crossed Chelsea Bridge.
17-01-2013 10:38 am	—	Grosvenor Rd.
17-01-2013 10:40 am	—	Sloane St: Royal Borough of Kensington and Chelsea.
17-01-2013 10:42 am	—	Pont St.
17-01-2013 10:46 am	—	Almost certain that parcel is in a delivery van. Movement is stop and go.
17-01-2013 10:52 am	—	Location is unchanged. Image is black.
17-01-2013 10:54 am	—	Parcel is almost there!
17-01-2013 10:57 am	—	Moving in the wrong direction now. Near Cardogan Square Gardens.
17-01-2013 11:03 am	—	Still not moving. Image is black. We expect delivery within next two hours.
17-01-2013 11:10 am	—	Moving closer towards Ecuadorian Embassy.
17-01-2013 11:40 am	—	Moving around slowly.
17-01-2013 11:46 am	—	On Pavilion Rd.

and switching off the camera
instead through the
unmanned photography
we also received
pictures of places
ordinarily hidden from view
for instance pictures
of the inner life
of the postal system"

"A global conflict
is emerging
all round the Embassy"
Carmen says
"the world's powers
the governments
are exploiting the Internet
for total surveillance
but at the same time
they're afraid of it
the threat of
total transparency
'We open governments
everywhere'
that is WikiLeaks'
slogan
and since you can't
turn back the clock
this conflict is escalating
and there
right behind Harrods
you can see
with your own eyes
this conflict that is mostly
only unfolding through
online media
police everywhere
antennas
walkie-talkies

vans
with tinted windows
Assange
is a symbol of this conflict
how can we
intervene into this space?
That's what we asked ourselves
what happens
if we try to transport
normality
into this space?"

Science fiction writer
Bruce Sterling
the grey eminence
of cyberpunk literature
wrote in "Wired"
"I see that the net.art
interventionist contingent
haven't lost
all their teeth yet"

Almost two months later
on 14 March 2013
a photograph
cropped up on the Internet
that had been smuggled
out of the prison cell
of 29-year-old
Per Gottfried Svartholm Warg
Svartholm Warg's moniker is
Anakata
he's one of the founders
of Pirate Bay a website
a kind of Google
for downloading music and film
legally
and illegally
and was hounded

17-01-2013 12:28 pm — Dear Postman. This is the way to go. It is only 0.5 miles to Ecuadorian Embassy. Please deliver.

by Hollywood
for which he's doing two years
solitary confinement
in Sweden
one of the messages
Assange held up
to the camera was
"Free Anakata"
and in answer
Anakata
now held up
a card
to the camera
"Free Assange"

Fondue with Julian Assange

A few weeks
after the delivery
Doma and Carmen received
an invitation to dinner
from Julian Assange
in order to
talk about
ways and means
of continuing the work
"Julian had let us know"
Carmen says
"that he would like
to accept our offer
of sending the parcel
on to someone
in a similar situation"

As far as the meal
was concerned
Doma and Carmen offered
to do the cooking
and Assange replied

17-01-2013 12:45 pm — Inside view of postbag.

"Bring what you fancy"
they met
at the Ecuadorian
Embassy
for fondue
because usually foreigners
are delighted
when you serve them
fondue
as Carmen had already done
for friends
in Venezuela
or in Paris

Two police officers
were posted
at the entrance to the building
two more
were standing guard
in the stairwell prepared
to arrest Julian Assange
the minute he should take a single step
out of the Embassy
to the right in the stairwell
the entrance
to the Colombian Embassy
to the left
you go to Ecuador
consisting of a single-story flat
Carmen rang the bell
and a security officer in civvies
opened the door
you had to walk through a metal detector
that was switched off
the man compared the passports
with the names
that had been announced
"Welcome to Ecuador" he said
and scanned

17-01-2013 1:27 pm — Parcels and letters inside van.

the cheese
we'd brought along
from Switzerland
and the fondue pot
and white wine
and the head of lettuce
and the beet salad
and then Assange
was standing at the door
he moves
and lives
and works
in two of the
eleven rooms
of the Embassy
small
but high rooms
full of computers
and laptops
and mobiles
and file folders
and legal matters
asylum applications
his Australian election campaign
blocking credit cards
WikiLeaks
Sweden
a fitness treadmill
books
the meditations
of Roman Emperor
Marcus Aurelius
an oxygen tank
and a breathing mask
in case there's
a fire in the Embassy
and he still doesn't want to leave
a child's drawing
of Assange

17-01-2013 1:36 pm — Nearly empty.

hanging on to a rope
James Bond style
and suspended above
the Beefeaters
in their red uniforms

In those days on the street
to the Embassy there weren't just
police officers
there was also a poster
advertising the Hollywood flick
"The Fifth Estate"
a movie about WikiLeaks
that depicts
Assange
as a self-centred bad guy
and that
to Assange's satisfaction
turned out to be the biggest
flop amongst
the year's movies
"They claimed in the film
that I belonged to a sect
and that was why
I'd been dying my hair white
since my childhood"
Assange says
"and then they were surprised
that I didn't want to
meet the leading man
the script had been
leaked to us ahead of time
I saw
that the movie
was giving me a raw deal
I didn't want to
play
into their hands
as for me

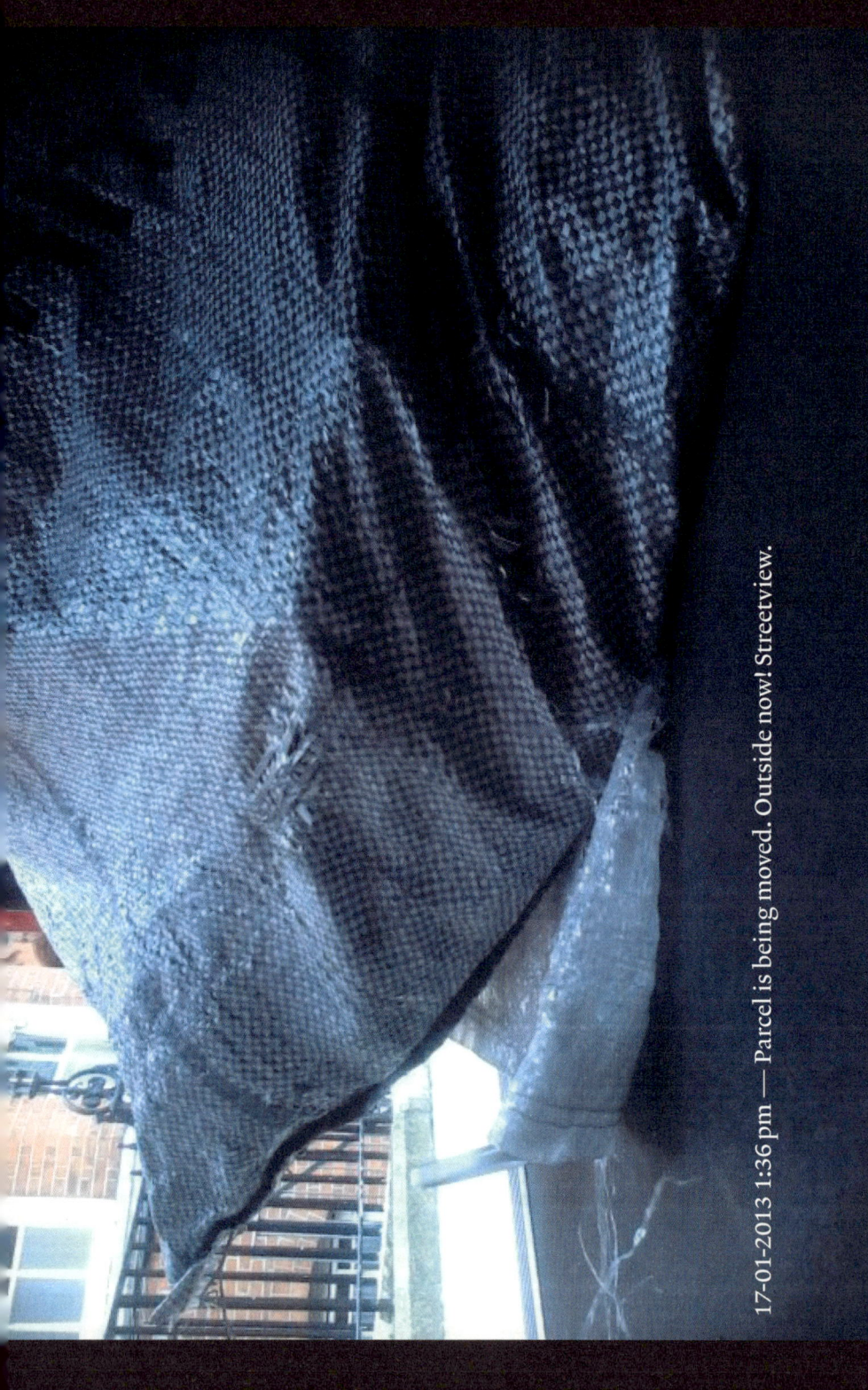

17-01-2013 1:36 pm — Parcel is being moved. Outside now! Streetview.

they could have cancelled
the entire film
instead
they cut the only scene
that I liked
in the original script
there was an exchange
in which an official
of the US State Department
told a staff member
to call Visa Amazon MasterCard
immediately and
cancel all of
WikiLeaks' bank connections
and the employee
replied
'We can't do that
we're in America'"
and then Assange laughed
he was in a good mood
and that was astonishing
somehow
because in order to be left
in peace that evening
he'd had to pull the curtains
so that the officers
on the street
couldn't stare in
through the windows

The good mood
was also astonishing
because to date
he still doesn't know
if or when the situation
is going to change
"And I don't want to talk
about it either"
he says

17-01-2013 1:44 pm — Something red is in front of camera now.

"because
given my situation
I'm constantly debating
which signals
to send out
to my friends
and therefore automatically
to my enemies
and I don't much feel like
talking about the weather
to me it is still
simply summer
like it was
the day
I stepped foot
in the Embassy"

A few hours later
the atmosphere
was not only good
it was positively
light-hearted
thanks to the white wine
we'd brought along
except for once when Assange
lost a chunk of bread
while stirring it
in the fondue
and Doma
a bit tipsy said
jokingly
"It's a tradition
in Switzerland
when you lose your bread
in the fondue
you have to run
round the house once
in your birthday suit"
followed by

17-01-2013 1:45 pm — Delivery folder? Delivery list?

embarrassed silence
nobody said anything
nobody laughed
and Assange said
"That was kind of cheeky"
and then
he smiled
and said
"actually I've been warned
about fondue
because three friends
knew somebody who died
shortly after
eating fondue"

Even if Assange can't
leave the Embassy
at least he isn't
isolated
there are usually people visiting
from WikiLeaks
or from his legal team
led by former Spanish
magistrate Baltasar Garzón
as well as other advisors
and friends
and celebrities
who visit him
"My first year
at the Embassy
was interesting"
Assange later said
to a Dutch
newspaper
"I had a lot of exciting visitors
director Oliver Stone
Lady Gaga
Italian writer Roberto Saviano
and !Mediengruppe Bitnik"

17-01-2013 1:47 pm —— We think we are in front of Embassy now. Image is black.
17-01-2013 1:50 pm —— All dark. Waiting for delivery.
17-01-2013 1:51 pm —— Must be directly in front of Embassy now. Image is black.
17-01-2013 1:54 pm —— Still black. Same location outside Embassy.
17-01-2013 1:57 pm —— Same location. All is dark. Waiting.
17-01-2013 1:59 pm —— Still nothing happening. Black.

Vivienne Westwood
brought a pinkish red Westwood bag
full of exclusive gifts

What with the white wine
flowing freely
along with the fondue
Assange at some point
suggested sending
the parcel under his name
via Lady Gaga
to Bradley Manning
who was about to
go on trial for passing
classified U.S. Army documents
on to WikiLeaks including
films that showed
US soldiers murdering
Iraqi civilians
and journalists from Reuters
with machine-gun fire
from a helicopter
on top of that
the communiqués showed evidence
of torture
hundreds of cases
committed
by foreign soldiers
and Manning was on trial
for passing them on
and Assange wanted to send
the parcel to him at court
as a "sign of solidarity"
he said
and then jumped up
and came back
with a bottle of whiskey
and when the bottle was empty
and Assange opened another one

17-01-2013 2:01 pm — Still nothing happening. Diplomatic crisis?
17-01-2013 2:04 pm — Lunch break?

Carmen thought it was time to leave
because Doma
drunk
kept getting louder
and shouting all over the place
about the madness of
universal surveillance
which has to be fought
and so on
we said goodbye
with big hugs
and outside Doma
drunk started hammering
on the surveillance van
"Is somebody in there?
open the damn door"
and Carmen said
"Let's get out of here quick"
which is what they did

A Parcel for Mr. Rajab

It was 23 June 2013
when Doma was already
on the way to take
a flight from Zurich to London
with a suitcase
containing the parcel
for Bradley Manning
the Lady Gaga plan
had died
instead Assange would
send it by overnight express
from the Embassy
directly to Bradley Manning
at court
then his mobile rang
it was the assistant of
Baltasar Garzón

17-01-2013 2:49pm — "@bitnk package has arrived and is now with Embassy security", says @wikileaks on Twitter!

the WikiLeaks lawyer
she said
something has come up
"have you seen the news?"
she asked
"yes" Doma said
according to the news
Edward Snowden
who had been dominating
the world headlines
for the past few days
was just leaving Hong Kong
with the help of WikiLeaks
and WikiLeaks' employee
Sarah Harrison
possibly heading for Moscow
later it turned out
that the provisional
Ecuadorian passport
that had enabled Snowden
to leave Hong Kong
even though his US passport
had been annulled
hadn't even been issued by
Ecuador's Foreign Ministry
but by an Embassy
and not just any old Embassy
but the one in London
and the opposition in Ecuador
claimed that
Julian Assange
was controlling
the country's foreign affairs
and should be kicked
out of the Embassy
in any case
Garzón's assistant said
to Doma on the phone
the timing

17-01-2013 3:44 pm — The parcel camera transmitted over 9000 images. Most of them are black.
17-01-2013 3:54 pm — Parcel camera has been online for 25 hours now. We estimate that batteries will last another 6 hours.

for sending
Bradley Manning
a parcel
couldn't be worse

"We've just worked nonstop
for two weeks"
Doma said
having already checked in
and cancelling the trip
at the last minute
"but it actually is better
to postpone the plan
Edward Snowden
is now sitting in a plane
to Moscow
attention is currently focused
someplace else
and that's exactly
what this kind of work involves
not knowing where it will lead us
in our work we also
want to show
what the treatment of people
like Snowden and Assange
does to them
like for instance
radically reducing their options
their freedom of movement
their freedom of action"

On 23 September
we met at the Embassy again
to work out how to proceed
"it's a relief
to see friends again"
Assange said
warmly kissing
Carmen on the cheek

17-01-2013 4:41 pm — Parcel still in Embassy waiting for security check. It looks like it is placed on a sofa.

and hugging Doma
and apologizing
for possibly being
a bit distracted
it was a personal affair
at the Super Bowl
the singer M.I.A.
sitting next to Madonna
had given the camera
the finger
and now the NFL
wanted to slap
a $1.5 million fine on her
so she wanted to
discuss it with
Assange
to get his device
they're close friends
M.I.A. called Assange's
mobile
three times
within the next hour
and he stood in a corner
of the room
and whispered
in his inimitable way
so you couldn't understand
a single word

In the meantime
Bradley Manning
had been sentenced
to 35 years in prison
and would be eligible
for parole
only after serving
eight years
the day after he was sentenced
Manning had issued

17-01-2013 6:04 pm — First view of a room in the Embassy!

a statement
that in the future
he wanted to be perceived
as a woman
his new name
Bradley wrote
was Chelsea Manning
and Assange felt that
restraint was in order
media attention would not help
Chelsea at the moment
"I think
it would harm her"
Assange said
"if she received
a package from me now"

It would be better
Assange said
to send the package to
Nabeel Rajab
whose release
he had demanded
on one of the cards
he wrote when he received
the Bitnik parcel
"Rajab"
Assange said that evening
"is a human rights activist
sitting in jail
because he used political means
to fight an authoritarian monarchy
that is supported
by the United States
because he criticized
the king's uncle
on Twitter
and in contrast
to many others

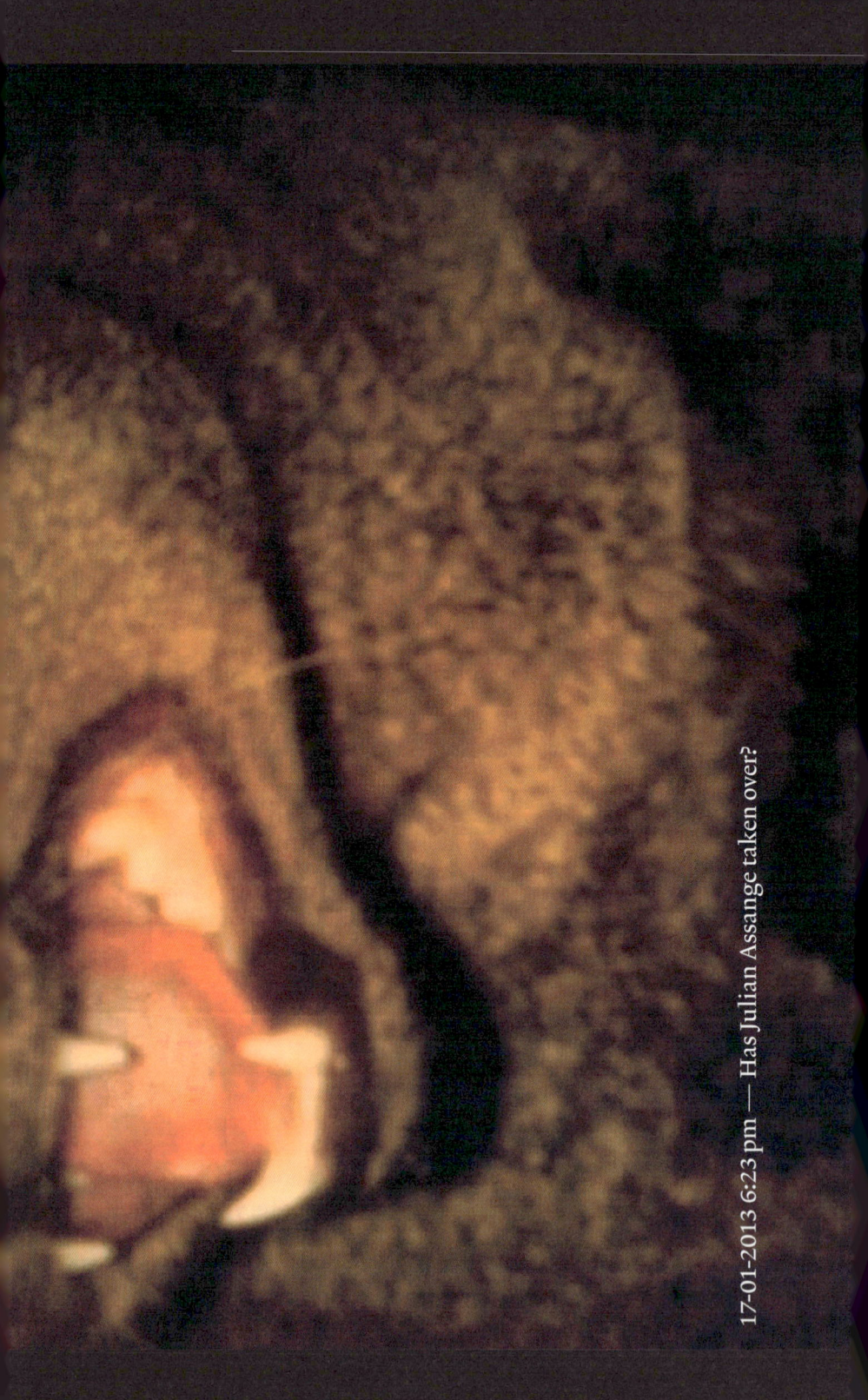

17-01-2013 6:23 pm — Has Julian Assange taken over?

Nabeel Rajab
has been ignored by the media
which is one of the reasons
he is still
imprisoned"

"I know him personally"
Assange then said
"Nabeel came to see me
in England in 2012
I was producing
the program 'World Tomorrow'
for 'Russia Today'
some of my guests were
Hassan Nasrallah
Slavoj Žižek
Rafael Correa
and
Nabeel
on the way to England
he tweeted that
he was meeting me to do
an interview for a TV show
whereupon 100 police officers
with machine guns
surrounded his family's house
in Bahrain
and when he came back
from England
he was arrested"

And because Julian Assange
speaks in clear simple slogans
like a good copywriter
and being an activist wants
messages to strike home
and come across
crystal clear
he added

— Is this thing on! Hello Julian Assange! We are here!

17-01-2013 6:25 pm

"Nabeel Rajab
is Bahrain's
Nelson Mandela"

Together we drank
a bottle of
Dalwhinnie Single Malt
and decided
to send the parcel
by Royal Mail
at the end of October
"End of October is good"
Assange said
"I've always got
a crowded agenda
but I won't be
involved in
anything major then
and I'm here anyway
of course you never know
if something or other
is going to come up
at the last minute
you know
things happen"

Sender
Julian Assange
Ecuadorian Embassy
3 Hans Crescent
London
SW1X OLS GB
Addressee
Nabeel Rajab
Jaw Prison
Hawar Highway
Jaw Bahrain 317
Bahrain
Telephone 0097 317 84 31 11

17-01-2013 6:30 pm — Some kind of wild cat image.

So on Monday
28 October 2013
Carmen and Doma showed up
along with Adnan
the parcel
with the modified mobile
wrapped in gift paper
to avoid potential issues
with Embassy security
the security guard
collected all mobiles
standard procedure
recently
bugs had been discovered
at the Embassy
anyway
on that Monday
in October
Julian Assange had
a cold
and the blue
Veterans for Peace hoodie
and the baseball cap
of the Sea Shepherd Conservation
Society
and the bottle of Glenfiddich
twelve years old
and the police officer
in front of the window
and a hoarse voice
when he said
"Okay so now
let's arm this thing"

Assange Can't Go Out Bitnik Can't Go In

"You don't really feel
the whole project
until you've sat

Hello World!

and stared at a black screen
for twenty hours"
Doma said
and the second parcel
was different
from the first
where the whole thing practically
ran without a hitch
but then, of course, the sender was
!Mediengruppe Bitnik
and the parcel was sent
from London to London
this time the sender was
Julian Assange
the addressee was in Bahrain
in a maximum security prison
so the game rules had changed
first of all
after the parcel was picked up
at the Embassy
in addition to the mobile Assange
had put appeals from
Human Rights Watch
and Amnesty International
in the parcel
calling for
Nabeel Rajab
to be released
so first thing
the Embassy staff
went ballistic
because they had explicitly said
that no parcel
shooting pictures
can ever enter or leave
the Embassy again
and even though Juan
a staff member of WikiLeaks
had carefully draped a cloth

17-01-2013 6:40 pm — Julian Assange's performance from the Ecuadorian Embassy.

over the parcel
so that there really would be no
pictures taken inside the Embassy
the fact that there was
a package again
was all it took
even though the mobile
did not take a single picture
through the hole
in the cardboard
until it had been carried
to the delivery van
in other words when it was no longer
on Ecuadorian territory
the security guard
went bonkers
and then the ambassador
went bonkers
and said in a rage
!Mediengruppe Bitnik
would never be allowed
to enter the Embassy again
and a few weeks later

Doma and Carmen
actually were turned away
when they wanted to visit Julian
but then two hours later
there was a call
and the caller said
"you can enter the Embassy again
but only
if you permit yourselves to be frisked
head to toe
and do not bring
any electronic devices
along
absolutely none
not even a calculator

— Welcome to Ecuador.

or an MP3 player
not even
a USB stick
nothing"
but first thing to begin with
the ambassador was in a snit
shortly after the package
had left the Embassy
and had been driven
to Camden
to the headquarters of Parcelforce
the company commissioned by
the Royal Mail
to transport the package

There
the parcel simply stayed put
although it
had been sent
overnight express
it didn't stay put for an hour
or two or three
but for 24 hours
and after a sleepless night
he hadn't eaten anything
either
since the performance had started
"I can't eat
in situations like that"
Doma said
he was still staring
nonstop
at the screen
at the GPS signal
that hadn't moved one iota
for twenty hours
just staring
in the London hackspace in Hackney
where he had installed himself

17-01-2013 6:49 pm —— Justice for Aaron Swartz – Julian sitting at table.

the hackspace is a room
that has everything you need
when you want to work
with electronics
with laser cutters
or 3D printers
or if you want build
a toaster
or bugs
or an entire computer
men and women
between eighteen and sixty
were sitting at eight tables
and at the neighbouring table
fifty-year-old John was working
on a hacked
oversized
laser-driven
knitting machine
full of drill holes
that looked
like you could
fly to the moon with it
this is the world
that Julian Assange
comes from
the world of computer nerds
and hackers
and activists
and exactly the right place
to stare apathetically
and now and then
euphorically
at a screen
without someone
asking what it is
that you're doing
Carmen
was video chatting

17-01-2013 6:51 pm — Free Bradley Manning.

from Zurich
and so Doma said
"When you've stared
 at a black screen
for twenty hours
you slowly begin
feeling the project"

100-Hour War of Nerves

Hardly had he said that
after almost 24 hours
of no action
when the GPS signal
suddenly started
jumping
and Doma jumped up
and shouted "movement"
and Adnan switched
the camera on
the Parcelforce status
reported
the package
had been passed on
to FedEx
but the GPS signal
wasn't moving
in the direction of Heathrow
Doma and Carmen had assumed
it would be loaded
onto an aircraft in Heathrow
or that
it would be held up
and that was
the more realistic possibility
at security
because actually
there's not much chance of
a switched-on mobile

17-01-2013 6:51 pm — Free Nabeel Rajab.

passing through security
above all
in a parcel
full of cables and batteries
that looks like a bomb
but now
the parcel was moving
anyway
and in an entirely different direction
from the airport
and stood still for ten minutes
in fact right in
the middle of a motorway
and the traffic indicator
on the Internet
was glowing green
meaning open roads
red means a traffic jam
but the indicator was glowing green
"Why is the damned parcel
standing still
in the middle
of the motorway?"
Doma
shouted and then asked
more to himself than anybody else
"So what do we tweet now?"

But Carmen
had already taken over in Zurich
she tweeted
"on the move
Camden Finsbury Tottenham
next stop Bahrain?"
shortly afterwards
Assange tweeted
to two million
followers
on WikiLeak's Twitter

17-01-2013 6:52 pm — Free Anakata.

"Live-parcel to @NabeelRajab
is on the move again
next stop Bahrain?
#postdrone"
suddenly
the signal
took a big leap
to the edge of the city
the coordinates showed
Stansted Airport
a small airport
on the outskirts of London
and the GPS coordinates
specified in Google Maps
zoomed
to a gigantic building
large letters saying
FedEx International

In his former life Felix worked
as a digital forensics specialist
if you have
deleted all of the data
on your computer
Felix could find them
and maybe
you'd end up with a problem
now Felix was responsible for
keeping Bitnik's server
up and running
in case there was too much traffic
then he would simply
use other servers
and in between
to pass the time
between two bottles of Club Mates
it had taken him five minutes
to program an alarm
in case

17-01-2013 6:52 pm — Free Jeremy Hammond.

Doma had wanted
to take a short nap
which he didn't
but if he had
an alarm on the computer would have
woken him up
with a song by rapper
Schoolboy Q
the minute the parcel's GPS
coordinates
had shifted noticeably

But that wasn't the issue at this point
because Felix was combing
the Internet
to find all the cargo aircraft
scheduled to leave
Stansted
within the next 24 hours
and concluded
from his research
that the route from Stansted
to Bahrain
had to go via Paris
"We have to keep an eye on
flights to Paris" he said
but then the following happened
nothing

The parcel stayed in Stansted
overnight
which meant that
after 48 hours
it was still in London
and Adnan
placid as a Zen Buddhist
and with a knack
for asking the right questions
at the wrong time

17-01-2013 6:53 pm — Free Rudolf Elmer.

wanted to know from Doma
whose nerves were predictably frayed
after two sleepless nights
"Incidentally
will the Sim card
work in Bahrain?"
"Yes yes"
Doma said
he had activated the card
for various countries
and via Skype
he and Carmen
gave the American magazine "Wired"
and "Al Akhbar" from Lebanon
an interview
they all wanted to talk
to Bitnik
about the political aspect
of the whole story
in contrast to the journalist
from the "Tages-Anzeiger"
all she wanted to know
was what Assange
usually has for breakfast
"Whiskey"
Doma could've said
but he didn't
and Assange tweeted
"live package from #Assange
to political prisoner
@NabeelRajab
mysteriously held
at airport
for almost
24 hours"

And then the worst possible
thing happened
in Doma's view

17-01-2013 6:54 pm — Free Anons.

at least in the tunnel view
he had acquired
after staring at the screen
for 60 hours
the parcel did move
but unfortunately
in the wrong direction
instead of leaving
the country in an airplane
the signal followed
the exact same route
back to where it had come from
to the Parcelforce warehouse
in Camden and
agreement was unanimous
probably back to
Julian Assange
and because the GPS left
a red line
everywhere the parcel went
better than
in the first delivery
followers could see
dozens of lines
crisscrossing London
marking the path
of the parcel
which should have left
the country long ago

After three days
on Thursday
the atmosphere had deteriorated
Juan from WikiLeaks
who had carried
the parcel out of the Embassy
was worried about trouble
with the ambassador
on that same day

17-01-2013 6:57 pm — Transparency for the state! Privacy for the rest of us!

Assange had not set foot
outside the Embassy
for 500 days
on the same day
the German politician
Christian Ströbele
visited
Edward Snowden
in Russia
while an American congressman
said about the
practices of the NSA
"You can't have
your privacy violated
if you don't know
your privacy is violated
right?"

In the meantime
Carmen
had called FedEx
where a man claimed
that the package was at Parcelforce
and Parcelforce claimed
FedEx had it
of course Carmen
could have told them
"I know exactly
where it is
latitude 51.538279
and longitude −0.134792"
but then
the answer would have been
a parcel
that sends signals
can't be loaded onto a plane anyway
and that would have been
the end of the mail art piece
everybody was on edge

17-01-2013 6:58 pm — Postal art is contagious!

Doma shouted
and Carmen shouted
and Carmen said
"we'd better have no contact
for a couple of hours"
and embarrassed Adnan
said nothing
and Felix hammered away
at the keyboard
and Carmen and Doma
glared at each other
through the video chat
and because
there was nothing to do
Doma
sent a public twitter message
to Parcelforce's customer service
and CCed WikiLeaks
a shot
in the dark
that was at 3:49 pm
"@parcelforce
hi
we sent a parcel
to Bahrain
on Monday
It still seems to be
in London
what happened?"

At 5:13 pm
after it had been carted
from Parcelforce to FedEx
and from there back
to Parcelforce
the parcel was
driven back
to FedEx
in Stansted

17-01-2013 6:59 pm — Thank you Ecuador.

and Julian Assange sent
a two-part tweet
"One can imagine
the politics
as the political
hot-potato parcel
is thrown
between Royal Mail
Parcelforce
FedEx and UK Customs
no one
wants to be
left holding the parcel
if a story breaks
about refusing
to let it through
to Bahrain's
top political prisoner"

And then
only three hours later
when according to the
Parcelforce status update
the parcel had left the country
the GPS signal
suddenly vanished
for seven minutes
briefly reappeared
and disappeared again
"we're airborne" Felix said
then a blackout
for 58 minutes
then the signal
cropped up again
and the new coordinates
logged into Google Maps
led to
"Charles de Gaulle
Paris"

17-01-2013 7:01 pm — Thank you to all our supporters.

After a two-hour
stopover
the signal disappeared again
reappearing
a couple of hours later
the GPS
had now drawn
a gloriously
long red line
from London
to Paris
to Dubai
in the United Arab Emirates
only
one hour flying time away
from Bahrain

"Foreign Policy" wrote
"Meanwhile
WikiLeaks founder Julian Assange
has launched something of
a gonzo activist project
sending a package
to the imprisoned
Bahraini activist
Nabeel Rajab
complete with a camera
a GPS tracker
and appeals for his release
The package is described as a
'live mail art piece'
and through a hole in the box
is documenting its journey with photos
taken from the camera inside the box
The package looks to have just left
London's Stansted airport
though according to WikiLeaks
it was 'mysteriously' held there
for 24 hours"

17-01-2013 7:02 pm — Keep fighting!

Cyber Hippie Philosophy

Doma said
"the action
is just taking too long
loss of control is too great
I keep underestimating
the loss of control
in our actions
even when this loss of control is exactly
what we're looking for
when we planted bugs
at the Zurich Opera
or hacked
the surveillance cameras
in the London Underground
and challenged security
to a game of chess
or when
at the height of
the financial crisis
we displayed
'UBS lies'
on an illuminated billboard
outside a London
exhibition space
or when we built
the very first
pirate TV station
in Jamaica"
"the effect"
Carmen says
"is always the same
you throw a wrench
into the system
intervene
open a channel of
communication
and wait for a reaction

the outcome of
the live experiment
is as unpredictable for us
as it is for viewers
and that's
what I like about this kind of art
the conscious loss of control"

Which means in this case
that Doma has
been on his feet
for 130 hours
"This action reflects
the spirit of the cyber hippies
in the seventies
in every respect"
he says
"namely
that the human body
is just a bother
bodies
want to sleep
and eat
and be in a bad mood
but actually
all I want is
to process information
nonstop
without sleeping
I want to be one single
information processing machine
at the same time
it is exactly in this same spirit
we intervene artistically
in Bahrain
without being there
in other words
without endangering
our own bodies"

17-01-2013 7:06 pm — Julian Assange.

Then
the chances
that the parcel
would reach its destination
were poor
because Nabeel Rajab
is sitting in a gaol
because parcels
with electronic devices
that send signals
have a hard time
getting through security anyway
so then
from one second
to the next
at customs in Dubai airport
on Saturday morning
8:55 am London time
and 12:55 pm Dubai time
after a five-day journey
just like that
with no warning
with no explanation
"We don't know
what happened"
FedEx later claimed
without having made it
to Bahrain
to Nabeel Rajab
sitting in gaol
for having criticized the monarchy
and without the picture
of a security officer
tearing open the parcel
and staring into the camera
the GPS signal of the parcel
for Nabeel Rajab
from Julian Assange
went dead

Dubai, 25 November 2013: On a Friday in November, Adnan and Doma, coming from London and Zurich, flew to Dubai. To try again. They wanted to mail the parcel for Nabeel Rajab in Dubai, take the next plane and the minute they were in the air, Carmen would start live-tweeting from Zurich. "I was nervous with all the electronic gear in my suitcase but we passed through customs with no trouble at all," Doma said a few weeks later, when they met with Assange to sum things up over raclette and white wine.

Carmen had brought cheese along again from Switzerland, two kilogrammes, and pickled onions, bacon, white wine and a raclette grill, accepted by Embassy security and not rejected as an "electronic device".

"The entire city," Doma said, "seemed a little like a huge airport. Skyscrapers, cameras, deserted streets – surveillance architecture. It is very, very quiet in the underground. You barely dare to speak. To me Dubai was like a city of the living dead, and every ten metres a photograph of the Sheikh."

"The future," Assange said.

Doma and Adnan had holed up in a hotel for two days. They tried to swim in the sea but access was privatized everywhere and it cost $75. At the airport they discovered a gigantic FedEx building. "After checking the GPS data, it turned out," Doma said, "that contact with the first parcel had been lost in that same FedEx building." They posted the parcel at a post office and took the next plane out. Then Carmen started tweeting.

"#Postdrone is back online. Starting a second attempt. Delivery for Mr. Rajab. http://rajab.bitnik.org/live.html #postdrone @wikileaks @NABEELRAJAB"

Twenty hours later. Hardly had the parcel arrived at airport cargo when the signal vanished again and Carmen tweeted, "Dubai Airport seems to be a bad place for our postdrones. Second parcel to @nabeelrajab has been missing

17-01-2013 7:08 pm — View from inside the Ecuadorian Embassy.

for 48h." And later, "Dubai. The great firewall for Bahrain. Still no news about second parcel to @nabeelrajab. It disappeared at Dubai customs 3 weeks ago."

First Edition, 27 February 2014
Copyright © 2014 Echtzeit Verlag GmbH, Basel
All rights reserved

ISBN 978-3-905800-81-4

Supported by: Helmhaus Zürich, Stadt Zürich Kultur

Tweets, Images and Text:
Copyleft 2014 !Mediengruppe Bitnik, all rights reversed
http://wwwwwwwwwwwwwwwwwwww.bitnik.org/assange/
http://rajab.bitnik.org/

Author: Daniel Ryser, !Mediengruppe Bitnik
Editing: Armin Büttner
Translations from the German: Catherine Schelbert
Copyediting: Birgit Althaler
Design: Müller+Hess, Basel
Printing: Ebner & Spiegel, Ulm

www.echtzeit.ch

17-01-2013 7:18 pm — Black.
17-01-2013 7:31 pm — This was a LIVE Mail Art Piece by !Mediengruppe Bitnik featuring Julian Assange.
17-01-2013 7:37 pm — Thanks and goodbye!

Julian Assange war erkältet
seine Stimme war heiser
und zwei Oktaven
tiefer als sonst
trotzdem
sprach er an diesem Tag
nicht so leise
wie er das sonst häufig tut
manchmal
spricht er so leise
da denkt man
man wird verrückt
da hängt man
total konzentriert
an seinen Lippen
und versteht
trotzdem nur die Hälfte
und glaubt schon
an einem Gehörschaden zu leiden
und fragt sich
ob er absichtlich so spricht
in dieser aussergewöhnlichen Situation
so dass vielleicht
kein Richtmikrofon
herausfiltern kann
was er gerade sagt

Julian Assange
war also
an diesem Montag
Ende Oktober 2013
erkältet
und seine Stimme
heiser
er trug
ausgewaschene Jeans
und einen blauen Kapuzenpullover
der Veterans for Peace
und eine schwarze Baseballcap

16.01.2013 12:38 — Schlangestehen im Postamt.

der Sea Shepherd Conservation Society
die Jagd macht
auf die Jäger von
Walen
und Robben
und Delfinen
Assanges Frühstück
bestand an diesem Vormittag
zunächst
aus einem grossen Schluck
Glenfiddich Single Malt
zwölf Jahre alt

Er räusperte sich
die Stimme klang nun
nach dem ersten Schluck
voller
weniger heiser
er nahm
einen zweiten Schluck
«Whiskey»
sagte er dann
«ist das beste Mittel
gegen Erkältung»
und draussen
vor dem Fenster
stand ein Londoner Polizist
und Assange lächelte
und sagte
«also gut
dann lasst uns
das Ding
scharf machen»

«Das Ding»
ein Paket
im Inneren
ein Handy so präpariert
dass die Kamera

alle zehn Sekunden
ein Bild schiesst
durch ein kleines Loch
in der Kartonwand
und dieses Bild
live ins Netz überträgt
und das Handy-GPS
gibt im selben Zehn-Sekunden-Takt
den Standort des Pakets durch
dazu kommen
sechs Batterien
gekoppelt an den Handy-Akku
für wochenlange Sendezeit

«Den Anfang der Aktion»
sagt Carmen
«machte eine Pizza»
in Ecuador
machte sich im August 2012
der Aussenminister daran
zu verkünden ob
Julian Assange
Asyl erhalten werde
oder nicht
Assange
in Schweden konfrontiert
mit Vorwürfen
zwei Frauen
sexuell belästigt zu haben
war vor einem internationalen Haftbefehl
in die ecuadorianische Botschaft
in London
geflüchtet
verkleidet
als Briefträger
so heisst es
um einer möglichen Auslieferung
an die USA zu entgehen
wo es gegen ihn

16.01.2013 12:44 — Angestellte nimmt Lieferung entgegen und steckt Paket in Postsack.

eine geheime Anklage geben soll
deren Inhalt
auch seine Anwälte
nicht kennen
und zahlreiche US-Politiker
liessen sich vernehmen
dass man Assange
wegen seiner Rolle
als WikiLeaks-Gründer
am besten
ohne Gerichtsverfahren
erschiessen soll
in London
umstellten Polizisten
die Botschaft
drohten
mit dem Sturm des Gebäudes
TV-Teams filmten
und sendeten im Internet
ohne Unterbruch
weltweite Aufregung

Carmen verfolgte
zusammen mit Doma
ihrem Mann
und Künstlerpartner
das Geschehen
im Atelier in Zürich
gemeinsam
sind sie das Kernteam
der !Mediengruppe Bitnik
sie sahen es über
«Reuters TV»
«Russia Today»
«Guardian»
Twitter
informierten sich
in verschiedenen Chats
zum Beispiel auf 4Chan

16.01.2013 12:44 — Innenleben eines Postsacks. Paket mit laufender Kamera unterwegs zu Julian Assange.

ein Forum
das Anonymität bietet
4Chan
so heisst es
sei die Wiege des Kollektivs
Anonymous
und in diesem Forum
verfolgten
hunderte Nutzer
das Geschehen in London
über Live-Streams
«Was können wir für Julian tun?»
fragte einer irgendwann
«Die haben bestimmt Hunger
in der umstellten Botschaft»
schrieb ein anderer
«Ich bestelle denen mal eine Pizza»

Ein paar Minuten später
sahen Doma und Carmen
und alle
die auf welchem Sender auch immer
das Geschehen verfolgten
wie auf einem Motorrad
ein Kurier
von Domino's Pizza Service
vorfuhr
sich ein wenig wunderte
warum hier
so viele Polizisten herumstehen
sich dann an den Beamten vorbeidrängte
an der Botschaftstür klingelte
und mit einem Sicherheitsbeamten
diskutierte
der ihm klarzumachen schien
hören konnte man es ja nicht
dass hier niemand
eine Pizza bestellt hatte
und kurz darauf

16.01.2013 15:32 — Wohin als Nächstes? Inzwischen haben wir Julian Assange über Lieferung informiert.

erschien ein weiterer Kurier
und dann noch einer
ein völliges Durcheinander
Weltpresse
Polizisten
Assange
WikiLeaks
internationale
diplomatische Krise
und Pizza von Domino's

Und dann
an diesem 16. August 2012
erklärte Ecuadors Aussenminister
Ricardo Patiño
ebenfalls live auf Sendung
dass Julian Assange
in den USA
kein faires Verfahren erwarten könne
und dass man ihm deshalb
Asyl gewähre
das kleine Ecuador
14 Millionen Einwohner
der Weltmacht die Stirn bietend
in Südamerika
kann man
mit solchen Symbolen
einen Wahlkampf gewinnen
und vor der Botschaft in London
brachen WikiLeaks-Unterstützer
in Jubel aus

«Was können wir jetzt tun?»
fragte ein Nutzer auf 4Chan
«Ein Taxi»
schrieb ein anderer
«Julian braucht nun ein Taxi
zum Flughafen
damit er von dort

16.01.2013 15:57 —— Schwarzes Bild seit 15:33. Zweifel: Hat womöglich jemand Kamera zugeklebt?
16.01.2013 16:08 —— Schwarz. Aber ein Blick auf die GPS-Daten zeigt: Paket bewegt sich.
16.01.2013 16:27 —— Paket nun nahe Haggerston Park, East London.
16.01.2013 17:24 —— Paket in Bewegung. Hackney Central. East London. Bild: Schwarz. Kamera futsch?
16.01.2013 17:34 —— Schwarz. Schwarz. Schwarz. Paket im East London Mail Centre in Whitechapel.

nach Ecuador reisen kann»
und kurz darauf
fuhren vor der Botschaft in London
ein Dutzend Taxis vor
und schwarze Limousinen
mit «Mr. Assange»-Schildern
in den Frontscheiben
und in der engen Strasse
vor der Botschaft
brach der Verkehr zusammen

«Es waren grandiose fünf Stunden»
sagt Doma
«Es war einerseits das Live-Erlebnis»
sagt Carmen
«Du sitzt vor dem Computer
und weisst nicht
was als Nächstes passiert
weil irgendwo
Kids vor dem Computer sitzen
und sich überlegen
wie sie in das Geschehen
eingreifen können»
sagt Doma
«Andererseits» sagt Carmen
«waren die Taxis
die Limousinen
die auf Assange warteten
der zwar soeben Asyl erhalten hatte
aber keinen Schritt
vor die Botschaft machen durfte
auch ein politischer Kommentar
Taxis vorbeischicken
live auf allen Kanälen
ist zudem ein sehr persönlicher Eingriff
mitten in ein geopolitisches Ereignis
plötzlich fühlten wir alle
die auf 4Chan herumhingen
und den Weg 13

16.01.2013 19:28 — Lichtschimmer! Paket im Hauptverteilerzentrum Mount Pleasant.

von der Pizza-Bestellung
zum Auftauchen der Pizza-Kuriere
verfolgt hatten
als hätten wir gemeinsam
der abstrakten Geopolitik
unsere persönliche Geschichte
entgegengestellt»

«Während Occupy Wallstreet
zum Beispiel» sagt Carmen
«malten die Leute Schilder
warum sie selbst
ein Teil jener 99 Prozent seien
der hoch verschuldete Student
der zu kurz gekommene Rentner
die vielleicht gar nicht viel
gemeinsam hatten
aber sich
mit einem persönlichen Anliegen
zu einem Protest
der 99 Prozent
vereinten»

So entstand die Idee
Julian Assange
ein Paket zu schicken
ein Paket mit präpariertem Handy
damit wie bei einer üblichen
Live-Übertragung
jede und jeder im Netz
den Weg des Pakets
verfolgen konnte
von der !Mediengruppe Bitnik
kuratiert und kommentiert
auf dem eigenen Twitter-Account
in Fast-Echtzeit
als Live-Ticker
von einer Postannahmestelle
in Hackney

16.01.2013 20:30 — Kamera in bester Ordnung! Perfekte Innenansicht des Hauptverteilerzentrums.

bis hin zur Botschaft von Ecuador
Flat 3B 3 Hans Crescent
direkt hinter
dem Luxuseinkaufszentrum Harrods

Der Mann aus Guatemala

Doma baute drei Wochen
an dem Paket
präparierte das Handy
testete die Batterien
die Live-Übertragung
über einen Mittelsmann
Mike von der Aktivistengruppe
The Yes Men
nahmen Doma und Carmen
Kontakt auf mit Leuten
aus dem engen Umfeld
von Assange
«Es ging uns dabei
einzig darum
ihn wissen zu lassen
dass da was kommt»
sagt Carmen
«Wir wollten nicht
dass sich die Botschaft
oder Assange
bedroht fühlten
denn das Paket
kann im Scan
für eine Bombe
gehalten werden
mit dem Handy
und den Drähten
und den Batterien»

In der Nachricht
die sie Assange
zukommen liessen

16.01.2013 20:32 — Hinten Rollbehälter, im Vordergrund ein Förderband.

schrieben
Carmen und Doma
«Wenn du
das Paket erhältst
könntest du bitte
1. Uns deine Sicht
auf die diplomatische Krise zeigen
die sich rund um die Botschaft
abspielt
2. Das Paket weiterschicken
an eine Person
deiner Wahl»

Anfang Januar
kam über einen Kontaktmann
einen Aktivisten aus Guatemala
in einem verschlüsselten Chat
über das Netzwerk Tor
wo nichts und niemand
Spuren hinterlässt
eine knappe Nachricht
«Julian ist einverstanden»
nicht mehr
aber auch nicht weniger

«Wir wussten nicht
wie Julian reagieren würde»
sagt Doma
«Wir wussten nicht einmal
ob das Paket so weit kommt
ich flog von Zürich nach London
baute in Adnans Wohnung
drei identische Pakete
zwei davon
waren Ersatzpakete
falls das erste
abgefangen werden sollte
Adnan
gehört auch zu Bitnik

16.01.2013 20:33 — Aussicht aus dem Rollwagen.

er hält unsere Arbeit
seit zehn Jahren auf Film fest
hunderte Stunden Material
keine Ahnung
was daraus werden soll
ich stellte also in Adnans Küche
einen verschlüsselten
Videochat-Kanal her
zu Carmen in Zürich
und
wenn er nicht gerade
in der Krippe war
oder schlief
zu unserem Sohn Leano
von Küche zu Küche
der Kanal war immer offen
drei Tage lang»

Nach einer ersten
schlaflosen Nacht
gab Doma das Paket
in einem indischen Kiosk
in Hackney auf
noch auf dem Weg zur Post
korrigierte er
einen letzten Fehler
der Software
er hatte im letzten Moment bemerkt
dass das Handy
nach tausend Fotos
abstürzt
und sich ausschaltet
insgesamt würden es am Schluss aber
über zehntausend Bilder sein
auf dem ersten Bild
um 12:38
sieht man Doma
wie er sich mit dem Paket
in einem Spiegel in der Annahmestelle

16.01.2013 20:45 — Beine.

fotografiert
um 12:44 verschwand das Paket
in einem roten Postsack
und ab da
sendete die Kamera
stundenlang
schwarz

Kaum war das Paket aufgegeben
begann Carmen zu twittern
auf dem für diese Aktion
eingerichteten Account
Followerzahl
zu diesem Zeitpunkt
null
der erste Tweet
am 16. Januar 2013 um 12:30
lautete
«Wir senden Julian Assange
ein Paket mit Kamera
die Kamera dokumentiert die Reise
durch das Postsystem in Echtzeit
#Assange»

Schnell gab es erste Retweets
«Und kurz darauf
wurde unser Server
überrannt» sagt Carmen
«Unser Rechner
erhielt nicht mehr hundert Anfragen
pro Minute
sondern 30 000
er stand kurz vor dem Kollaps»
«Ich habe in den folgenden Stunden
von der Aussenwelt
nichts mehr mitbekommen»
sagt Doma
«Zwei Tage habe ich
die Wohnung nicht verlassen

16.01.2013 20:58 — Mann mit Bart schiebt Rollwagen. Geschäftiges Treiben.

36 Stunden war ich
ununterbrochen
in diesem Film
zwei Nächte lang
ständig hatte ich Angst
dass unser System abstürzt
dass etwas schiefläuft
gleichzeitig
erzählten wir auf Twitter
die Geschichte der Reise
organisierten
zusätzlich neue Server
denn unser überlasteter Server
schickte nun ständig
Fehlermeldungen
und redeten mit Journalisten
ich fühlte mich
wie ein Dampfkochtopf
kurz vor der Explosion»

«@bitnk
hallo
hier ist Dave von der
Technik-Abteilung
von BBC News
erlaubt Ihr uns
die Bilder zu verwenden?»
«Vice»
«La Stampa»
«Ars Technica»
«Huffington Post»
Globo
«El Comercio»
«Nation of Swine»
das Schweizer Radio
«und die Mutter
von Julian Assange
äusserte über Twitter
ihre Begeisterung» sagt Doma

16.01.2013 20:59 — Paket wird bewegt. Sicht auf Halle leicht verändert.

«Wir wurden überrollt»
sagt Carmen
«wir wussten ja nicht
ob überhaupt jemand
ausser uns
die Aktion wahrnehmen
oder die Sache
interessant finden würde»

Auf Twitter
und in Internetforen
starteten
Diskussionen
auf der Plattform
«Hacker News» zum Beispiel
«Ich denke
dies ist eine schlechte Idee»
schrieb einer
«wenn Royal Mail
von der Sache Wind kriegt
werden sie das Paket
zerstören»
jemand antwortete
«Und das soll schlecht sein?
Ich denke nicht
dass sie ein Problem haben
mit möglicher Sachbeschädigung
sie wollen ja vor allem
herausfinden
was passiert»

Im Schritttempo zur Botschaft

Um 17:16
sendete das Paket
kein Signal mehr
das Bild schwarz
und Doma überfiel Panik
«Verdammt

16.01.2013 21:07 — Zurück im Postsack. Diesmal grün.

ist es das schon gewesen?»
nachdem er
verzweifelt
eine Stunde lang
auf einen schwarzen Bildschirm
gestarrt hatte
glaubte Doma plötzlich
eine Veränderung
erkennen zu können
«Hat sich nicht soeben
das Schwarz
ein wenig verfärbt?»
fragte er Adnan
«ist es jetzt
nicht eher hellschwarz?»

Signal und Bewegung
um 18:01
von East London
zu einem Verteilerzentrum
in der Innenstadt
ins Mount Pleasant Mail Centre
das Handy hatte wohl
in einem Funkloch gesteckt
die Botschaft rückte näher
dafür brach nun
wegen der steigenden Zugriffe
der Server zusammen
kaum hatten Doma und Carmen
das Teil wieder zum Laufen gebracht
und die Leistung endlich
auf mehrere Server verteilt
meldete sich die Kamera
mit Bildern zurück
das erste Bild
aus dem Postsystem
eine hell erleuchtete Lagerhalle
in Whitechapel
Männer beim Verladen von Paketen

16.01.2013 22:34 — Totale Dunkelheit. Aber GPS-Daten verändern sich. Jetzt auf Kings Cross Rd.
16.01.2013 22:35 — Paket bewegt sich schnell. Grays Inn Rd.
16.01.2013 22:37 — Weiterhin schwarz. Kings Cross Station.
16.01.2013 22:43 — Euston Road Richtung Regent's Park.
16.01.2013 22:45 — Marylebone Rd.
16.01.2013 22:50 — A40. Schnell.
16.01.2013 22:53 — Paket wohl in Lieferwagen. A40 nahe East Acton Station.
16.01.2013 23:04 — Hangar Ln. Jetzt Gunnersby Av.
16.01.2013 23:08 — Great West Rd. Jetzt Hogarth Ln.
16.01.2013 23:12 — Great Chertsey Rd, Hounslow.
16.01.2013 23:18 — Twickenham Rd, Richmond.
16.01.2013 23:25 — Hampton Rd E, Feltham.
16.01.2013 23:29 — Godfrey Way, Hounslow.
16.01.2013 23:33 — Ankunft Ceva Logistics, Godfrey Way, Feltham.

Handwagen hin und her schiebend
um 21:07 wurde das Paket
in einen grünen Postsack umgeladen
bevor es dann
vor Mitternacht
weiterreiste
jedoch nicht
in Richtung Botschaft
sondern in eine völlig andere
raus aus der Innenstadt
raus aus London

«Warum? Warum? Warum?»
brüllte Doma und
rauchte fünf Zigaretten
und Adnan
der wegen der Aktion
ganz vergessen hatte
dass er vor ein paar Stunden
seinen Studenten
ein Seminar hätte geben müssen
kochte ihm einen Beruhigungstee
Carmen
zugeschaltet per Videochat
war überzeugt
dass das Paket nun
wo auch immer
zerstört würde
es bewegte sich 22 Kilometer
nach Heathrow
dort blieb es dann
und man sah wieder nur schwarz
gegen 2:30 nachts
sah man kurz einen Fuss

Aber dann
wurde das Paket nicht gesprengt
stattdessen wurde es
frühmorgens

um 5:32
zurück ins Zentrum gefahren
in ein neues Verteilerzentrum
in unmittelbarer Nähe zur Botschaft
«Warum bringt man ein Paket
dessen Ziel im Zentrum liegt
zuerst raus nach Heathrow
und dann wieder zurück?»
fragte jemand auf Twitter
«Ich sehe da bei der Post
Optimierungspotenzial»
eine andere Followerin twitterte
«Was ich von @bitnk
gelernt habe:
Pakete verbringen
ihre meiste Zeit
in totaler Dunkelheit»

Nach einer weiteren
schlaflosen Nacht
sah Doma
wie sich das Paket
am 17. Januar
um 10:34
wieder in Bewegung setzte
das GPS-Signal wanderte
in Richtung Botschaft
dann aber
schon fast da
nur ein paar hundert Meter noch
bewegte es sich
nur noch
ganz
langsam
im Schritttempo
zwei Stunden lang
war es ständig fast
in Griffnähe zur Botschaft
ohne anzukommen

17.01.2013 03:07 — Paket hat London verlassen. Ceva Logistics, nahe Flughafen Heathrow.

«Kann es sein
dass euch der Postbote
auf Twitter folgt
und ein feines Gespür
für Spannung hat?»
twitterte einer
durch die Bilder
die die Kamera jetzt lieferte
konnte man erkennen
dass man sich tatsächlich
in einem Lieferwagen
der Post befand
eine Tür
die auf und zu ging
das Innere eines Wagens
voller Pakete
die immer weniger wurden
bis irgendwann
man sah es nun auf den Bildern
fast nur noch
dieses eine Paket übrig war
und als das Paket
nach zwei Stunden
noch immer
nicht ausgeliefert war
wurden die Zuschauer
vor den Bildschirmen
langsam unruhig

«Hey Bitnik
wann wird dieses Paket
endlich abgeliefert?
Ich sollte wirklich langsam
anfangen zu arbeiten»
«Beeilung Bitnik
niemand in meinem Büro arbeitet
das Paket hat bereits
meinen Morgen ruiniert»
«Ich beobachte diese Sache

17.01.2013 03:10 — Verdammt. Schon wieder schwarz.

seit 24 Stunden
langsam
kann ich nicht mehr»
«Ich habe soeben
den ganzen Tag damit verbracht
ein Paket
auf seinem Weg nach Ecuador
zu beobachten
es ist total faszinierend
aber ich weiss echt nicht wieso»
«Das ist aufregender
als der Mars-Rover»
und Marina Galperina
von «Animal New York»
bloggte zeitverschoben
«Was bedeutet dieser
Paket-Blitzkrieg?
Was befindet sich sonst noch
in diesem mysteriösen Paket?
Und warum
kann ich nicht aufhören
auf die ständig auf
Schwanzhöhe gefilmten
Räume
irgendeiner
ausländischen Poststelle
zu starren?
Warum
machen
diese Twitter-Updates
derart süchtig?»

Dann ging der Postbote
in die Mittagspause

Die Minuten
kamen Doma und Carmen
völlig übermüdet
wie sie waren

17.01.2013 06:06 — Guten Morgen London!

nun wie Stunden vor
die Erlösung
sie kam eine Stunde später
um 14:04
nach 25 Stunden auf Adrenalin
und zwar
in Form eines Tweets
von @wikileaks
«Live-Kamera
per Post verschickt
zu Assange
das GPS-Signal
sendet nun
aus dem Lieferwagen
direkt vor der Botschaft
@bitnk»
«Da wussten wir»
sagt Carmen
«sie nehmen die Aktion wahr
sie spielen mit
spätestens da
war ich dermassen nervös
als müsste ich
einen Vortrag halten
vor 15 000 Leuten
und irgendwie
haben wir ja auch
einen Vortrag gehalten
vor 15 000 Leuten»
Doma antwortete
«@wikileaks
könnt
ihr
den
Wagen
sehen?»
@wikileaks antwortete
«Wird der MI5
das Paket öffnen?»

17. 01. 2013 08:27 —— Unscharfe Lichtquelle: Paket zurück in Postsack?
17. 01. 2013 08:32 —— Fast wieder ganz dunkel, aber Bewegung.
17. 01. 2013 08:34 —— Lichtblitze.
17. 01. 2013 08:38 —— Bild wieder dunkel. Nun nahe Battersea Park, London.
17. 01. 2013 08:53 —— Vereinzelte Lichtblitze. Mehrheitlich schwarz.
17. 01. 2013 09:29 —— Stillstand in Vauxhall. Lieferwagen im Stau? Bild: schwarz.

Eine halbe Stunde später
um 14:49
schrieb @wikileaks
«@bitnk
das Paket ist angekommen
und befindet sich nun
bei der Botschaftssicherheit»

Grosser Jubel
in Adnans und in Carmens Küche
und auf Twitter auch
nur ein ehemaliger Londoner Postbote
beschwerte sich per Mail
er habe in einem
der vom Paket
durchquerten Verteilerzentren
zehn Jahre lang
am Sicherheitsscanner
gearbeitet
niemals
wirklich niemals
hätte er dieses Paket
durchgelassen

«Willkommen in Ecuador»

Dann blieb die Lieferung liegen
eine Stunde
zwei Stunden
drei
auf Twitter
wurde währenddessen
von hunderten Usern
niedergeschrieben
was Doma und Carmen
hofften
oder fürchteten
alle Möglichkeiten
wurden durchgespielt

17.01.2013 09:49 — Im Royal Mail Jubilee Mail Centre ausserhalb Londons.

«Ich bin ziemlich sicher
die sprengen
das Ding in die Luft
es sieht einfach
zu krass aus»
und «die Chancen stehen
nach wie vor sehr gut
dass wir heute noch
Julian Assanges Lächeln
zu sehen bekommen»
und «startet eine Massenhysterie»
und «womöglich hättet ihr
etwas Feines zum Essen
ins Paket legen sollen
dann hätte er es womöglich
schon längst geöffnet»
und «die letzten
fünfzig Schritte
sind immer die härtesten»
und vor allem
«bitte lass jetzt
die Batterie
nicht sterben»

«Julian
erzählte uns später»
sagt Carmen
«das Paket
habe tatsächlich
eine kleine Krise ausgelöst
die damalige Botschafterin
fürchtete Probleme
welcher Art auch immer
wenn Fotos
vom Inneren der Botschaft
nach draussen dringen
oder sie fürchtete
den allgemeinen Wirbel
und sie verlangte

17.01.2013 09:50 — Snackautomat. Stuhl.

eine Freigabe
vom Aussenminister persönlich
erst als Assange
ihr klargemacht habe
BBC
berichte live über die Aktion
da habe die Botschafterin
grünes Licht gegeben»

Um 18:19
streckte plötzlich
ein Berglöwe
seinen Kopf
in die Kamera
oder ein Bombenspürhund?
Dann ein Teppich?
Ein lederbezogenes Sofa?
«Ich war schon
auf der Botschaft
ich erkenne dieses Sofa wieder»
schrieb eine Journalistin
und der offizielle Twitterer
der «Huffington Post»
verlor nun die Nerven
«Julian winke uns zu!
Julian Julian winke uns zu!»

Eine beschriftete Karte
wurde ins Bild gehalten
«Läuft dieses Ding?»
dann eine zweite
«Hello world»
Und dann
erschien
Julian Assange
im Bild
in einem Pullover
von WikiLeaks
er lächelte

17.01.2013 09:51 — Was ist jetzt los? Wird hier der Inhalt unseres Pakets diskutiert?

und hielt
weitere Karten
in die Kamera

«Willkommen in Ecuador»
«Freiheit für Bradley Manning»
«Freiheit für Nabeel Rajab»
«Freiheit für Anakata»
«Freiheit für Jeremy Hammond»
«Freiheit für Rudolf Elmer»
«Freiheit für Anonymous»
«Gerechtigkeit für Aaron Swartz»
«Transparenz für den Staat!
Privatsphäre für uns andere!»
«Paketkunst ist ansteckend!»
«Danke Ecuador»
«Danke allen Unterstützern»
«Kämpft weiter»
«2013 gewinnen wir!»
«Ende!»
«Keine Karten mehr!»

Das Bild
wurde wieder schwarz
wie schon unzählige Male
in den Stunden zuvor
als nicht klar war
ob das Paket
in einem Mülleimer landet
oder beim MI5
«Weil spätestens
nachdem WikiLeaks sich
über Twitter geäussert hatte
alle Geheimdienste
dieser Welt
von dieser Kunstaktion wussten»
wie Carmen sagt
eine Aktion
die Julian Assange

festgesetzt in einer Wohnung in London
fast filterlos in die Wohnungen
tausender Zuschauer transportierte
fast hatte man das Gefühl
man habe ihn jetzt persönlich
kennengelernt

@WeRAllAnonymous twitterte
«vielen Dank
an die Künstler der
!Mediengruppe Bitnik
für die beste Twitter-Unterhaltung
aller Zeiten
wir salutieren vor euch!»
Christine Assange
Julians Mutter
schrieb
«es ist wunderbar
Julian lachen und den Moment
geniessen zu sehen
wie die #Assange
Botschafts-Paketkamera
von @bitnk
heute gezeigt hat
kann künstlerische Kreativität
eine aussergewöhnliche
politische Kraft entfalten»
und jemand twitterte
«yeah
@bitnk
hat heute definitiv
das Internet gewonnen»

«Nun wieder Dunkelheit»
twitterte Doma
als Assange
nach seiner Performance
aus dem Bild verschwand
und das Bild

wieder schwarz wurde
um 19:31 Londoner Zeit
am 17. Januar 2013
twitterte Carmen
zum Abschluss der nun
32 Stunden andauernden
Live-Übertragung
für die tausenden Zuschauer
die das Geschehen
auf der Bitnik-Webseite
und auf Twitter
live verfolgten
sie twitterte so
als sei dies alles
nach einem Plan verlaufen
als sei die Assange-Performance
eine Selbstverständlichkeit gewesen
«Das war
eine Live-Mailart-Performance
der !Mediengruppe Bitnik
featuring Julian Assange
danke und gute Nacht!»
und in Adnans Küche
in Hackney
als sich der Adrenalinspiegel senkte
brach Doma
nach zwei schlaflosen Nächten
langsam zusammen

«Im Zeitalter
der totalen
digitalen
Überwachung
in der jede E-Mail
von der NSA gelesen wird»
sagt Doma
«wollten wir
das gute alte
noch immer bestehende

17.01.2013 10:07 — Im Rollwagen. Aber wohin? Zur Inspektion?

Postgeheimnis nutzen
um zu sehen was passiert
wenn wir Julian Assange
ein Paket schicken
ein Brief ist heute
besser geschützt als eine E-Mail
eine E-Mail
aus der Schweiz nach England
kann heute von verschiedenen Staaten
gelesen werden
bei einem Paket
ist das nicht so einfach
das Postgeheimnis verhindert
dass Pakete und Briefe
einfach so geöffnet werden
und trotzdem fragten wir uns
wird es tatsächlich abgeliefert?
Oder gefilzt?
Gesprengt?
Verwanzt?
Vom Geheimdienst gescannt?
Löst es einen Alarm aus?
Überwindet es die Schranken
die Assange
von der Aussenwelt trennen?
Wir hatten in der Tat
mit anderen Bildern gerechnet
mit einem Sicherheitsmann etwa
der das Paket öffnet
und die Kamera ausschaltet
stattdessen erhielten wir
durch die
unbemannte Fotografie
auch Bilder von Orten
die normalerweise
verborgen bleiben
zum Beispiel Bilder
aus dem Innenleben
des Postsystems»

17.01.2013 10:29 — Schwarz.
17.01.2013 10:34 — Bewegung. Und zwar schnell. Hartington Rd.
17.01.2013 10:37 — Paket überquert Chelsea-Brücke.
17.01.2013 10:38 — Grosvenor Rd.
17.01.2013 10:40 — Royal Borough of Kensington and Chelsea.
17.01.2013 10:42 — Pont St.
17.01.2013 10:46 — Langsame Fahrt mit vielen Stopps: Wir müssen im Auslieferwagen sein.
17.01.2013 10:54 — Paket ganz in Nähe von Botschaft!
17.01.2013 10:57 — Aber warum denn jetzt plötzlich in die falsche Richtung? Umdrehen!
17.01.2013 11:03 — Schwarz. Erwarten Lieferung in den nächsten zwei Stunden.
17.01.2013 11:10 — Sehr gut: Bewegung geht wieder in Richtung Botschaft.
17.01.2013 11:40 — Kreuz und quer durch das Viertel. Und sehr, sehr langsam.
17.01.2013 11:46 — Pavilion Rd.

«Rund um die Botschaft
manifestiert sich
ein globaler Konflikt»
sagt Carmen
«Die Mächtigen dieser Welt
die Regierungen
nutzen das Internet
für totale Überwachung
aber gleichzeitig
fürchten sie
die drohende
völlige Transparenz
‹Wir öffnen Regierungen
überall›
das ist der Slogan von
WikiLeaks
und weil sich das Rad
nicht zurückdrehen lässt
eskaliert dieser Konflikt
und dort
direkt hinter dem Harrods
kann man diesen Konflikt
der eigentlich nur medial
ausgetragen wird
mit eigenen Augen sehen
Polizei ist überall
Antennen
Funkgeräte
Wagen
mit abgedunkelten Scheiben
Assange
ist ein Symbol dieses Konfliktes
wie können wir
in diesen Raum eindringen?
Das haben wir uns gefragt
was passiert
wenn wir versuchen
Normalität in diesen Raum
zu transportieren?»

17.01.2013 11:50 — Weiterhin Pavilion Rd. Aber Licht! Tür des Wagens geht auf.

Science-Fiction-Autor
Bruce Sterling
die graue Eminenz
der Cyberpunk-Literatur
schrieb im «Wired»
«Ich sehe
die Interventionisten
unter den Netzkünstlern
haben ihren Biss
offensichtlich
noch nicht ganz verloren»

Fast zwei Monate später
am 14. März 2013
tauchte im Internet
ein Foto auf
das aus der Zelle
des 29-jährigen
Per Gottfried Svartholm Warg
geschmuggelt worden war
Svartholm Wargs Spitzname ist
Anakata
er ist einer der Gründer
der Seite Pirate Bay
eine Art Google für
Musik- und Film-Downloads
legale
und illegale
die von Hollywood
extrem unter Druck geriert
dafür sitzt er in Schweden
in Isolationshaft
für zwei Jahre
«Freiheit für Anakata»
hatte Assange
auf einer der Karten
gefordert
und Anakata
hielt jetzt

17.01.2013 12:28 — Und wieder zu. Lieber Postbote: Nur noch eine halbe Meile! Du hast es fast geschafft!

als Antwort
ebenfalls eine Karte
in eine Kamera
«Freiheit für Assange»

Ein Fondue mit Julian Assange

Ein paar Wochen
nach der Lieferung
erhielten Doma und Carmen
von Julian Assange
eine Einladung zum Essen
Ziel war es
zu diskutieren
wie man die Aktion
weiterführen könnte
«Julian hatte uns wissen lassen»
sagt Carmen
«dass er gerne
unser Angebot annehmen würde
das Paket
weiterzuschicken
an einen Menschen
in einer ähnlichen Situation»

Was das Essen anging
boten Doma und Carmen Assange an
etwas zu kochen
und dieser liess ausrichten
«Bringt worauf ihr Lust habt»
weil Ausländer in der Regel
entzückt sind
wenn man ihnen
ein Fondue auftischt
wie das Carmen für Bekannte schon
in Venezuela
oder in Paris
getan hat
traf man sich

17.01.2013 12:45 — Das aufregende Leben einer Postlieferung.

in der ecuadorianischen
Botschaft
zum Fondue

Zwei Polizisten
standen vor dem Eingang des Hauses
im Treppenhaus
wachten zwei weitere Polizisten
allzeit bereit
Julian Assange zu verhaften
sobald er auch nur einen Fuss
vor die Botschaft setzen würde
rechts im Treppenhaus
befindet sich der Eingang
zur kolumbianischen Botschaft
links
geht es nach Ecuador
in Form einer einstöckigen Wohnung
Carmen klingelte
und ein Sicherheitsmann in Zivil
öffnete die Tür
man schritt durch einen Metalldetektor
der ausgeschaltet war
der Mann verglich die Pässe
mit den im Vorfeld angemeldeten Namen
«Willkommen in Ecuador» sagte er
und scannte
den aus der Schweiz mitgebrachten
Käse
und das Fondue-Caquelon
und den Weisswein
und den Kopfsalat
und den Randensalat
und dann stand Assange in der Tür

Julian Assange bewegt sich
und lebt
und arbeitet
in zwei der insgesamt

17.01.2013 13:27 — Pakete. Briefe. Hand des Postboten. Wagen leert sich.

elf Zimmer
der Botschaft
kleine
aber hohe Räume
voller Computer
und Laptops
und Handys
und Ordner
mit juristischen Angelegenheiten
Asylverfahren
seiner australischen Wahlkampagne
Kreditkartensperrungen
WikiLeaks
Schweden
ein Fitness-Laufband
Bücher
die Selbstbetrachtungen
des römischen Kaisers
Marcus Aurelius
ein Sauerstofftank
und eine Atemmaske
falls es in der Botschaft brennt
und er auch dann
nicht raus will
eine Kinderzeichnung
wie Assange
in James-Bond-Manier
an einem Seil
über die rot gekleideten
Gardeinfanteristen
hinwegschwebt

In der Strasse zur Botschaft
begegnete man in jenen Tagen
nicht nur Polizisten
sondern auch einem Plakat
das für den Hollywood-Streifen
«The Fifth Estate» warb
einen Film über WikiLeaks

17.01.2013 13:36 — Jetzt ist fast alles ausgeliefert.

der Assange
als egozentrischen Bösewicht
darstellt
und später
zu Assanges Zufriedenheit
zum grössten Filmflop
des Jahres werden sollte
«Die behaupten in dem Film
ich sei Teil einer Sekte
und deshalb würde ich mir
seit ich ein Kind bin
die Haare weiss färben»
sagte Assange
«und dann wunderten sie sich
dass ich mich nicht
mit dem Hauptdarsteller
treffen wollte
wir hatten das Skript
vorab zugespielt bekommen
ich sah
dass ich im Film
extrem schlecht wegkomme
dieser Sache
wollte ich nicht
in die Hände spielen
von mir aus
hätten sie den ganzen Film
streichen können
stattdessen
haben sie
die einzige Szene gestrichen
die mir gefallen hat
im Original-Drehbuch
fand sich eine Stelle
in der ein Beamter
des US State Departement
zu einem Mitarbeiter sagte
‹Rufen Sie sofort
Visa Amazon Mastercard an

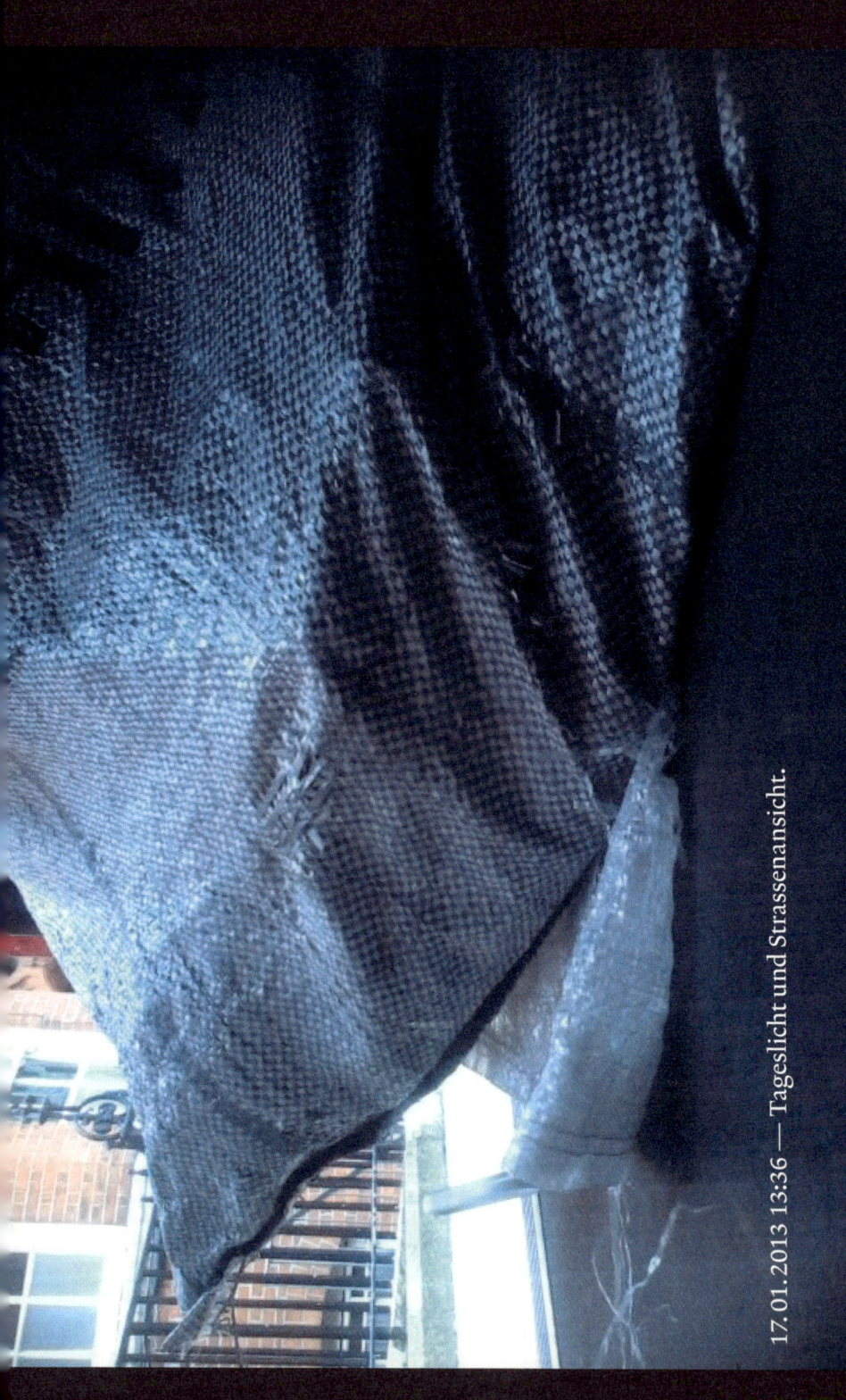
17.01.2013 13:36 — Tageslicht und Strassenansicht.

stornieren Sie
alle Bankverbindungen
von WikiLeaks›
und der Befehlsempfänger
entgegnete
‹Das können wir nicht machen
wir sind in Amerika›»
und dann lachte Assange
der gut gelaunt war
und das war irgendwie
erstaunlich
denn immerhin musste er
um an diesem Abend
ungestört zu sein
die Vorhänge zuziehen
damit die Polizisten
vor dem Fenster
nicht von der Strasse
reinglotzten

Erstaunlich
war die gute Laune
auch deshalb
weil er bis heute
nicht weiss
wann sich seine Situation
ändert
«und ich will darüber
auch nicht reden»
sagte er
«denn es ist
in meiner Situation
ein ständiges Abwägen
welche Signale
sende ich nach draussen
an meine Freunde
und somit automatisch
auch an meine Feinde
und über das Wetter reden

17.01.2013 13:44 — Zur Abwechslung rot.

will ich auch nicht
für mich ist draussen
einfach
nach wie vor
Sommer
so wie damals
an jenem Tag
als ich die Botschaft
betrat»

Ein paar Stunden später
war die Stimmung
nicht nur gut
sondern
dank dem mitgebrachten Weisswein
ausgelassen
einzig als Assange
beim Rühren
im flüssigen Fondue
ein Brotstückchen verlor
und Doma angetrunken witzelte
es sei Tradition in der Schweiz
dass der
der beim Fondue
sein Brot im Käse verliere
einmal nackt
ums Haus rennen müsse
da herrschte in der Runde
für einen Moment
betretenes Schweigen
niemand sagte etwas
niemand lachte
und Assange sagte
«Das war ziemlich frech»
und dann
lächelte er
und sagte
«Eigentlich war mir
von einem Fondue

17.01.2013 13:45 — Liste mit den Lieferungen des Tages?

abgeraten worden
denn drei Freunde hatten
je einen Bekannten der
kurz nach einem Fondueessen
gestorben ist»

Auch wenn er die Botschaft
nicht verlassen kann
so ist Assange zumindest
nicht isoliert
meistens sind Leute bei ihm
von WikiLeaks
von seinem Anwaltsteam
um den ehemaligen spanischen Richter
Baltasar Garzón
und andere Berater
und Freundinnen und Freunde
und Berühmtheiten
die ihn besuchen
«Mein erstes Jahr
in der Botschaft
war interessant»
sagte Assange später
gegenüber einer holländischen Zeitung
«Ich hatte viele spannende Besuche
Regisseur Oliver Stone
Lady Gaga
Schriftsteller Roberto Saviano
und die !Mediengruppe Bitnik»
und Vivienne Westwood
brachte eine rosarote Tüte
voller exklusiver Geschenke

Während zum Fondue
der Weisswein in Strömen floss
sprach sich Assange
irgendwann dafür aus
das Paket unter seinem Namen
über Lady Gaga

17.01.2013 13:47	Schwarz. Aber wenn das GPS-Signal nicht täuscht, stehen wir direkt vor der Botschaft.
17.01.2013 13:50	Dunkel. Wir warten. Geduldig.
17.01.2013 13:51	Schwarz. Vor der Botschaft.
17.01.2013 13:54	Nichts bewegt sich.
17.01.2013 13:57	Position unverändert.
17.01.2013 13:59	Dunkelheit.

an Bradley Manning zu schicken
dessen Prozess
damals kurz bevorstand
weil er vertrauliche Dokumente
der US-Armee
an WikiLeaks weitergegeben hatte
unter anderem Filme
die zeigten
wie US-Soldaten
aus einem Hubschrauber heraus
mit Maschinengewehrsalven
irakische Zivilisten
ermordeten
und Journalisten von «Reuters»
auch hunderte Fälle von Folter
durch ausländische Soldaten
belegten die Depeschen
für deren Weitergabe
stand Manning vor Gericht
und Assange wollte ihm das Paket
in den Gerichtssaal schicken
als «Zeichen der Solidarität»
sagte er
und dann sprang er auf
und kam zurück
mit einer Flasche
Whiskey
und als die Flasche leer war
und Assange eine zweite öffnete
wollte Carmen langsam gehen
weil Doma
betrunken
immer lauter wurde
und rumzubrüllen begann
vom Kontrollwahn
der alles umspannt
und den man bekämpfen müsse
und so weiter
man verabschiedete sich

17.01.2013 14:01 — Stillstand. Diplomatische Krise?
17.01.2013 14:04 — Mittagessen?

mit grosser Umarmung
und draussen hämmerte
der betrunkene Doma
gegen den Überwachungswagen
der Polizei
«Ist da wer drin?
macht die verdammte Tür auf»
und Carmen sagte
«Lass uns bloss schnell
von hier verschwinden»
und das taten sie dann auch

Ein Paket für Herrn Rajab

Es war der 23. Juni 2013
als Doma in Zürich
bereits unterwegs war
zum Flug nach London
in einem Koffer
das Paket
für Bradley Manning
der Plan mit Lady Gaga
war gestorben
stattdessen sollte Assange
von der Botschaft aus
das Paket
mit Overnight Express
direkt zu Bradley Manning schicken
in den Gerichtssaal
da klingelte sein Handy
es war die Assistentin
von Baltasar Garzón
dem WikiLeaks-Anwalt
sie sagte
etwas sei dazwischengekommen
«Habt ihr
die Nachrichten geschaut?»
fragte sie
«Ja» sagte Doma

17.01.2013 14:49 — «@bitnk Paket angekommen und in den Händen der Botschaftssicherheit», twitterr @wikileaks.

in den Nachrichten
hatte es geheissen
Edward Snowden
der seit ein paar Tagen
die Schlagzeilen der Welt dominierte
sei in dieser Stunde dabei
mit Hilfe von WikiLeaks
und mit WikiLeaks-Mitarbeiterin
Sarah Harrison an seiner Seite
Hongkong zu verlassen
womöglich in Richtung Moskau
es sollte sich sogar herausstellen
dass der provisorische
ecuadorianische Reisepass
der es Snowden ermöglichte
trotz annulliertem US-Pass
Hongkong zu verlassen
gar nicht vom Aussenministerium Ecuadors
ausgestellt worden war
sondern von einer Botschaft
und nicht von irgendeiner
sondern von jener in London
und die Opposition in Ecuador
behauptete
Julian Assange
kontrolliere
die Aussenpolitik des Landes
man solle ihn
aus der Botschaft werfen
auf jeden Fall
sagte die Garzón-Assistentin
an jenem Tag zu Doma am Telefon
sei es wirklich gerade
ein denkbar schlechter Zeitpunkt
Bradley Manning
ein Paket zu schicken
«Wir haben jetzt zwei Wochen
durchgearbeitet»
sagte Doma

17.01.2013 15:44 — Kamera im Paket hat bisher über 9000 Bilder gesendet. Mehrheitlich schwarze.
17.01.2013 15:54 — Kamera seit 25 Stunden online. Batterien sollten für weitere sechs Stunden reichen.

als er bereits eingecheckt
die Reise im letzten Moment abbrach
«Aber es ist in der Tat besser
die Sache zu verschieben
Edward Snowden
sitzt jetzt in einem Flugzeug
nach Moskau
der Fokus
liegt in den nächsten Tagen
ganz woanders
und genau das gehört
zu dieser Arbeit dazu
dass man nicht weiss
wohin sie einen führt
wir wollen mit unserer Arbeit
auch aufzeigen
was das Handeln von Leuten
wie Snowden und Assange
mit ihnen macht
wie es unter anderem ihre Optionen
massiv einschränkt
ihre Bewegungsfreiheit
ihren Handlungsspielraum»

Am 23. September
traf man sich erneut in der Botschaft
um das weitere Vorgehen zu besprechen
«Es tut gut
Freunde wiederzusehen»
sagte Assange
und küsste Carmen
herzlich auf die Wange
und umarmte Doma
und entschuldigte sich
falls er gerade etwas abgelenkt sei
es handle sich um eine private Geschichte
es ging um die Sängerin M.I.A.
sie hatte beim Superbowl
an der Seite von Madonna

17.01.2013 16:41 — Paket warret in der Botschaft weiterhin auf Sicherheitscheck. Sofastoff?

den Mittelfinger
in die Kameras gestreckt
und für diese Geste
verlangte nun die NFL von ihr
1,5 Millionen Dollar
Bussgeld
für einen gestreckten Mittelfinger
und darüber
wollte sie sich nun mit Assange beraten
die beiden sind eng befreundet
und in der folgenden Stunde
rief M.I.A.
dreimal
auf Assanges Handy an
und er stellte sich
in eine Ecke des Zimmers
und flüsterte
auf seine typische Art
ins Handy
so
dass im Zimmer
kein Wort zu verstehen war

Bradley Manning
war inzwischen
zu 35 Jahren Haft
verurteilt worden
mit ersten Aussichten
auf Bewährung
nach acht Jahren
und Manning
hatte inzwischen auch
in einem Schreiben mitgeteilt
er wollte künftig
als Frau wahrgenommen werden
sein neuer Name
schrieb Bradley
sei Chelsea Manning
und Assange war der Meinung

17.01.2013 18:04 — Erstes Bild aus der Botschaft.

man sollte nun Zurückhaltung üben
mediale Aufmerksamkeit
bringe Chelsea im Moment nichts
«Ich meine
es schadet ihr»
sagte Assange
«wenn sie jetzt
von mir ein Paket erhält»

Besser sei es
sagte Assange
man schicke das Paket
Nabeel Rajab
dessen Freilassung er
unter anderem
auf einer der Karten
gefordert hatte
als er das Bitnik-Paket bekam
«Rajab»
sagte Assange an diesem Abend
«ist ein Menschenrechtsaktivist
der im Gefängnis sitzt
weil er mit politischen Mitteln
ein autoritäres Königshaus bekämpft
das von den USA
unterstützt wird
er sitzt im Gefängnis
weil er auf Twitter
den Onkel des Königs kritisiert hatte
und im Gegensatz
zu vielen anderen
erhält Nabeel Rajab
keine mediale Aufmerksamkeit
was mit ein Grund ist
dass er noch immer
im Gefängnis sitzt»
«Wir kennen uns persönlich»
sagte Assange dann
«Nabeel hatte mich

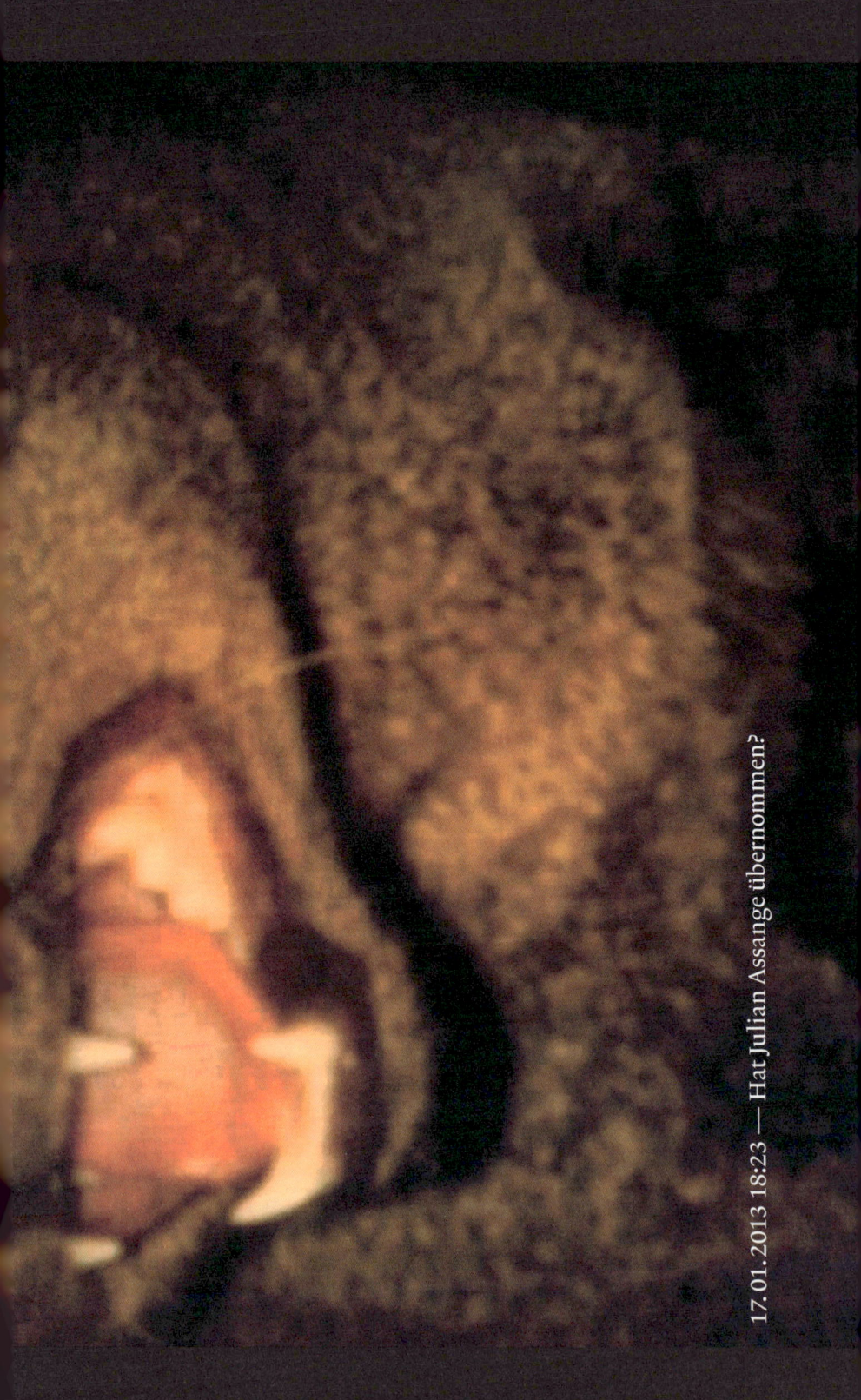

17.01.2013 18:23 — Hat Julian Assange übernommen?

im Mai 2012 in England besucht
ich produzierte für ‹Russia Today›
die Sendung ‹World Tomorrow›
meine Gäste waren
unter anderem
Hassan Nasrallah
Slavoj Žižek
Rafael Correa
und eben
Nabeel
auf dem Weg nach England
twitterte er
er treffe mich zum Interview
für eine TV-Show
daraufhin umstellten in Bahrain
100 Polizisten
mit Maschinenpistolen
das Haus seiner Familie
und als er aus England zurückkam
wurde er verhaftet»

Und weil Julian Assange
wie ein guter Werbetexter
in klaren einfachen Slogans spricht
und als Aktivist Botschaften
unmissverständlich
und zugespitzt
auf den Punkt bringen will
fügte er an
«Nabeel Rajab
ist Bahrains
Nelson Mandela»

Gemeinsam trank man
eine Flasche
Dalwhinnie Single Malt
und entschied
das Paket
Ende Oktober

Is this thing on?

17.01.2013 18:25 — Läuft dieses Ding? Natürlich läuft es! Hallo Julian Assange! Wir sind hier!

mit Royal Mail
loszuschicken
«Ende Oktober ist gut»
sagte Assange
«mein Kalender
ist zwar immer voll
aber dann bin ich
mit nichts Grösserem
beschäftigt
und ich bin ja
sowieso hier
natürlich weiss man nie
ob nicht noch
im letzten Moment
irgendwas dazwischenkommt
ihr wisst ja
Dinge passieren»

Absender
Julian Assange
Ecuadorian Embassy
3 Hans Crescent
London
SW1X OLS GB
Adressat
Nabeel Rajab
Jaw Prison
Hawar Highway
Jaw Bahrain 317
Bahrain
Telephone 0097 317 84 31 11

An jenem Montag also
dem 28. Oktober 2013
rückten Carmen und Doma an
zusammen mit Adnan
das Paket
mit dem präparierten Handy
in Geschenkpapier eingewickelt

17.01.2013 18:30 — Bild einer Raubkatze.

um mögliche Probleme
mit der Botschaftssicherheit
zu verringern
der Sicherheitsmann
sammelte die Handys ein
Standardprozedur
kürzlich
waren auf der Botschaft
Wanzen entdeckt worden
und Julian Assange war also
an diesem Montag
im Oktober
erkältet
im blauen Kapuzenpullover
der Veterans for Peace
mit der Baseballcap
der Sea Shepherd Conservation Society
und der Flasche Glenfiddich
zwölfjährig
und dem Polizisten
vor dem Fenster
und der heiseren Stimme
als er sagte
«dann lasst uns
das Ding
scharf machen»

Assange kann nicht raus
Bitnik kann nicht rein

«Das ganze Projckt fühlst du erst
wenn du zwanzig Stunden lang
auf einen schwarzen Bildschirm
gestarrt hast»
sagte Doma
und mit dem zweiten Paket
sollte es dann auch anders laufen
als mit dem ersten
beim ersten Paket

Hello world!

dort war noch alles
fast wie am Schnürchen gelaufen
aber da hiess der Absender auch
!Mediengruppe Bitnik
und das Paket wurde verschickt
von London nach London
jetzt hiess der Absender
Julian Assange
der Empfänger sass in Bahrain
in einem Hochsicherheitsgefängnis
und das hat das Spiel verändert

Zuerst einmal
nachdem der Kurier
das Paket in der Botschaft
abgeholt hatte
neben dem Handy hatte Assange
Aufrufe von
Human Rights Watch
und Amnesty International
ins Paket getan
die Nabeel Rajabs
Freilassung forderten
zuerst einmal
sind die Leute in der Botschaft
ausgerastet
weil sie doch klargemacht hatten
nicht noch einmal
dürfe hier ein Paket
rein oder raus
das Fotos schiesst
und auch wenn Juan
ein Mitarbeiter von WikiLeaks
extra ein Tuch über das Paket
gestülpt hatte
damit in der Botschaft
auch wirklich keine Aufnahmen entstehen
reichte der Umstand
dass da wieder ein Paket war

17.01.2013 18:40 — Die Performance von Julian Assange aus der ecuadorianischen Botschaft.

Und auch wenn das Handy
aus dem Loch
in der Kartonwand
tatsächlich erst Bilder schoss
als es vom Kurier
vom Hauseingang
zum Wagen getragen wurde
also nicht mehr auf dem Hoheitsgebiet
der Ecuadorianer
ist der Mann vom Sicherheitsdienst
ausgeflippt
und dann ist der Botschafter
ausgeflippt
in der ersten Wut
hat er gesagt
die !Mediengruppe Bitnik
dürfe die Botschaft
nie wieder betreten

Und tatsächlich
bei einem nächsten Besuch
ein paar Wochen später
wurden Doma und Carmen
zuerst abgewiesen
zwei Stunden später
kam dann ein Anruf
und der Anrufer sagte
«Ihr dürft wieder rein
aber nur
wenn ihr euch
von oben bis unten
filzen lasst
und keine
wirklich keine
elektronischen Geräte
in die Botschaft bringt
auch keinen Taschenrechner
auch keinen MP3-Player
nicht einmal

17.01.2013 18:42 — Willkommen in Ecuador.

einen USB-Stick
nichts»
aber zuerst einmal also
war der Botschafter richtig sauer
kurz nachdem das Paket
die Botschaft verlassen hatte
und vom Kurier
nach Camden gefahren wurde
ins Hauptlager der Firma Parcelforce
die den Auftrag von Royal Mail
übernommen hatte

Dort blieb das Paket
zuerst einmal
einfach liegen
obwohl es
aufgegeben war
als Overnight Express
es blieb nicht für eine Stunde liegen
oder zwei oder drei
sondern für 24 Stunden
und nach einer schlaflosen Nacht
gegessen hatte er
seit Beginn der Aktion
auch noch nichts
«Ich kann in solchen Momenten
nichts essen»
sagte Doma
starrte er noch immer
ununterbrochen
auf den Bildschirm
auf das GPS-Signal
das sich seit zwanzig Stunden
nicht gerührt hatte
Er starrte vor sich hin
im London Hackspace in Hackney
wo er sich eingerichtet hatte
der Hackspace ist ein Raum
wo man alles findet

17.01.2013 18:49 — Gerechtigkeit für Aaron Swartz – Julian sitzt an einem Tisch.

wenn man mit Elektronik
arbeiten will
mit Lasercuttern
oder 3D-Druckern
oder wenn man
einen Toaster bauen will
oder Wanzen
oder einen ganzen Computer
an acht Tischen
sassen Frauen und Männer
zwischen achtzehn und sechzig
und am Tisch nebenan
arbeitete der fünfzigjährige John
an einer überdimensionalen
aufgebohrten
gehackten
Strickmaschine
die aussah
als könnte man damit
zum Mond fliegen

Dies ist die Welt
aus der Julian Assange
gekommen ist
die Welt der Computernerds
und Hacker
und der Aktivisten
und genau der richtige Ort
um 24 Stunden apathisch
und dazwischen
immer mal wieder euphorisch
auf einen Bildschirm zu starren
ohne Gefahr zu laufen
dass sich irgendjemand
fragen könnte
was man hier tut
Carmen
war per Videochat
von Zürich zugeschaltet

17.01.2013 18:51 — Freiheit für Bradley Manning.

und Doma also sagte
«Wenn du zwanzig Stunden
auf einen schwarzen Bildschirm
gestarrt hast
dann fühlst du
das Projekt langsam»

100 Stunden Nervenkrieg

Kaum hatte er es gesagt
nach beinahe 24
regungslosen Stunden
sprang das GPS-Signal
plötzlich um
und Doma sprang auf
und brüllte «Bewegung»
und Adnan schaltete die Kamera ein
der Parcelforce-Status
meldete
das Paket
sei weitergegeben worden
an Fedex
aber das GPS-Signal
bewegte sich nicht
in Richtung Heathrow
davon waren Doma und Carmen ausgegangen
dass es in Heathrow
in einen Flieger geladen wird
oder aber
und das war
die realistischere Variante
dass es dort
beim Sicherheitscheck
aus dem Verkehr gezogen wird
weil eigentlich
stehen die Chancen schlecht
dass ein eingeschaltetes Handy
eine Sicherheitskontrolle passiert
vor allem

17.01.2013 18:51 — Freiheit für Nabeel Rajab.

wenn es in einem Paket steckt
das mit all den Drähten und Batterien
wie eine Bombe aussieht

Aber jetzt
bewegte sich das Paket sowieso
in eine ganz andere Richtung
als zum Flughafen
und blieb dann zehn Minuten stehen
und zwar mitten
auf einer Autobahn
und im Internet
leuchtete die Verkehrsführung grün
grün heisst freie Fahrt
rot heisst Stau
aber die Strecke leuchtete grün
«Warum steht das verdammte Paket
mitten auf der Autobahn?» schrie Doma
und dann fragte er
eher sich selbst als irgendwen anders
«Was sollen wir jetzt twittern?»
Carmen aber
hatte in Zürich schon übernommen
sie twitterte
«Unterwegs
Camden Finsbury Tottenham
nächster Halt Bahrain?»
kurz darauf
twitterte Assange
über WikiLeaks
an zwei Millionen Follower
«live-Paket an @NabeelRajab
ist wieder unterwegs
nächster Halt Bahrain?»
Plötzlich
machte das Signal
einen grossen Sprung
an den Stadtrand
die Koordinaten zeigten

17.01.2013 18:52 — Freiheit für Anakata.

Stansted Airport an
einen kleinen Flughafen
am Rande Londons
und die GPS-Koordinaten
bei Google Maps eingegeben
zoomten
ein riesiges Gebäude heran
beschriftet mit
Fedex International

Felix arbeitete in seinem früheren Leben
als digitaler Forensiker
wenn du
alle Daten auf deinem Computer
gelöscht hattest
konnte Felix sie finden
und vielleicht
hattest du dann ein Problem
jetzt war Felix dafür zuständig
die Bitnik-Server am Laufen zu halten
falls der Ansturm zu gross würde
dann würde er einfach
auf weitere Server ausweichen
und dazwischen
zum Zeitvertreib
zwischen zwei Club Mates
hatte er in fünf Minuten
einen Alarm programmiert
für den Fall
dass sich Doma
mal hätte schlafen legen wollen
was er dann zwar nicht tat
aber wenn er es getan hätte
dann hätte ihn ein Alarm am Computer geweckt
mit einem Song des Rappers
Schoolboy Q
sobald sich die GPS-Koordinaten
des Pakets
merklich verschoben hätten

17.01.2013 18:52 — Freiheit für Jeremy Hammond.

Aber das war jetzt gar nicht das Thema
denn jetzt durchsuchte Felix
das Internet
nach allen Frachtflugzeugen
die Stansted
in den nächsten 24 Stunden
verlassen würden
und bei seiner Recherche
kam er zum Schluss
dass der Weg von Stansted
nach Bahrain
nur über Paris
führen könne
«wir müssen die Flüge nach Paris
im Auge behalten» sagte er
aber dann ist Folgendes passiert
nichts

Das Paket blieb in Stansted über Nacht
und befand sich somit
nach 48 Stunden
noch immer in London
und Adnan
der die Gabe hat
mit der Gelassenheit eines Zen-Buddhisten
zum falschen Zeitpunkt
die richtigen Fragen zu stellen
fragte den nach zwei schlaflosen Nächten
sowieso schon nervlich angeschlagenen Doma
«Wird die Sim-Karte eigentlich
in Bahrain funktionieren?»
«Ja ja ja» sagte Doma
er habe die Karte
für verschiedene Länder freigeschaltet
und über Skype
gaben er und Carmen
dem amerikanischen «Wired»
ein Interview
und «Al Akhbar» aus dem Libanon

17.01.2013 18:53 — Freiheit für Rudolf Elmer.

sie alle wollten mit Bitnik
über die politische Dimension
der Aktion reden
eine Journalistin
des «Tages-Anzeigers» hingegen
wollte vor allem wissen
was Assange denn so frühstückt
«Whiskey»
hätte Doma sagen können
tat es aber nicht
und Assange twitterte
«Live-Paket von #Assange
für den politischen Gefangenen
@NabeelRajab
am Flughafen
mysteriöserweise
für 24 Stunden
zurückgehalten»

Dann passierte
in Domas Augen
das Schlimmstmögliche
zumindest in seinem Tunnelblick
den er nach 60 Stunden
auf Bildschirme Starren
entwickelt hatte
das Paket bewegte sich zwar
aber leider
in die falsche Richtung
es verliess nicht
im Flieger das Land
das Signal
bewegte sich zurück
dorthin wo es hergekommen war
auf der exakt gleichen Route
ins Parcelforce-Lager
in Camden
und von dort
darüber herrschte schnell Einigkeit

107

17.01.2013 18:54 — Freiheit für Anonymous.

wohl zurück zu
Julian Assange
und weil das GPS
besser als bei der ersten Lieferung
für alle Zuschauer im Netz sichtbar
auf einer Karte
rote Linien hinterliess
wohin immer es sich bewegte
zeichneten nun
nach zwei Tagen
dutzende Linien
kreuz und quer durch London
den Weg eines Pakets
das das Land
längst hätte verlassen haben sollen

Am Donnerstag
nach drei Tagen
war die Stimmung schlecht
WikiLeaks-Mitarbeiter Juan
der das Paket aus der Botschaft
getragen hatte
fürchtete Ärger
mit dem Botschafter
Assange hatte
an jenem Tag
die Botschaft
seit 500 Tagen
nicht mehr verlassen
am selben Tag
besuchte der deutsche Politiker
Christian Ströbele
Edward Snowden
in Russland
während ein US-amerikanischer Senator
über die NSA-Praktiken sagte
«Wie kann es ein Eingriff
in die Privatsphäre sein
wenn man es gar nicht merkt?»

17.01.2013 18:57 — Transparenz für den Staat! Privatsphäre für uns andere!

Carmen
hatte inzwischen Fedex angerufen
dort behauptete ein Mann
das Paket sei bei Parcelforce
und Parcelforce behauptete
es sei bei Fedex
natürlich hätte Carmen
den Telefonisten sagen können
«Ich weiss sehr genau
wo das Paket jetzt ist
Breitengrad 51.538279
Längengrad –0.134792»
aber dann
hätte die Antwort gelautet
ein Paket
das Signale sendet
dürfe sowieso nicht
in ein Flugzeug
und dann wäre die Aktion
beendet gewesen
die Nerven
lagen jetzt blank

Doma schrie
und Carmen schrie
und Carmen sagte
«Es ist besser
wir hören uns jetzt
ein paar Stunden nicht mehr»
und Adnan schwieg verlegen
und Felix hackte
auf die Tastatur ein
und Carmen und Doma
schwiegen sich im Videochat an
und weil es nichts zu tun gab
schrieb Doma dann
eine öffentliche Twitter-Nachricht
an den Parcelforce-Kundendienst
mit Kopie an WikiLeaks

17.01.2013 18:58 — Paketkunst ist ansteckend!

ein Schuss
ins Blaue
das war um 15:49

«@parcelforce
hallo
wir haben am Montag
ein Paket
nach Bahrain verschickt
es scheint aber noch immer
in London zu sein
was ist los?»

Um 17:13
nachdem es von Parcelforce
zu Fedex gekarrt worden war
und von dort
zurück zu Parcelforce
wurde das Paket
zurückgefahren
zu Fedex
nach Stansted
und Julian Assange verschickte
einen zweiteiligen Tweet
«Man kann sich
die politischen Ränkespiele
vorstellen
während die heisse Kartoffel
zwischen Royal Mail
Fedex
Parcelforce
und der UK-Zollbehörde
hin und her geschoben wird
niemand möchte die Verantwortung tragen
wenn bekannt wird
dass ein Paket
für den prominentesten
politischen Gefangenen Bahrains
zurückgehalten wird»

17.01.2013 18:59 — Danke Ecuador.

Und dann
nach nur drei weiteren Stunden
als das Paket
laut Status-Update
bei Parcelforce
das Land verlassen hatte
verschwand plötzlich das GPS-Signal
für sieben Minuten
tauchte kurz wieder auf
und verschwand wieder
«Wir sind in der Luft» sagte Felix
dann herrschte Funkstille
für 58 Minuten
dann tauchte das Signal
wieder auf
die neuen Koordinaten
bei Google Maps eingegeben
führten nach
«Charles de Gaulle
Paris»

Nach nur zwei Stunden
Zwischenlandung
verschwand das Signal wieder
um ein paar Stunden später
zurückzukehren
das GPS
hatte jetzt eine
wunderschöne
lange rote Linie gezogen
von London nach Paris nach Dubai
in den Vereinigten Arabischen Emiraten
nur noch eine Flugstunde entfernt
von Bahrain

«Foreign Policy» schrieb
«In der Zwischenzeit
hat WikiLeaks-Gründer Julian Assange
eine Art Gonzo-Projekt gestartet

17.01.2013 19:01 — Danke allen Unterstützern.

er schickte ein Paket
mit Kamera und GPS-Signal
auf den Weg nach Bahrain
zum gefangenen Aktivisten
Nabeel Rajab
und fordert dessen Freilassung
das Paket
wird als Mailart-Performance beschrieben
durch ein Loch in der Kartonwand
wird die Reise
fotografisch dokumentiert
das Paket
scheint den Flughafen
London Stansted
soeben verlassen zu haben
nachdem es dort
laut WikiLeaks
‹mysteriöserweise›
24 Stunden
liegen geblieben war»

Die Philosophie der Cyber-Hippies

Doma sagte
«Die Aktion
dauert schon viel zu lange
der Kontrollverlust ist zu gross
ich unterschätze den Kontrollverlust
bei jeder von unseren Aktionen
immer wieder von Neuem
auch wenn dieser Verlust genau das ist
was wir eigentlich suchen
als wir die Zürcher Oper verwanzten
oder Überwachungskameras
der Londoner Metro hackten
und die Security
auf ihren Bildschirmen
zum Schach aufforderten
oder als wir

17.01.2013 19:02 — Kämpft weiter!

auf dem Höhepunkt der Finanzkrise
ausserhalb eines Londoner
Ausstellungsraums
eine riesige beleuchtete Werbefläche
bespielten
mit dem Schriftzug
‹UBS lügt›
oder als wir auf Jamaika
den allerersten
Piratenfernsehsender
bauten»
«Der Effekt»
sagt Carmen
«ist immer derselbe
du schmeisst etwas ins System
schaffst eine Intervention
öffnest einen Kommunikationskanal
und wartest auf eine Reaktion
der Ausgang des Live-Experiments
ist für uns genauso völlig offen
wie für den Betrachter
und das ist es
was ich an dieser Art von Kunst mag
dieser bewusste Kontrollverlust»

Was in diesem Fall bedeutet
dass Doma nun
seit 130 Stunden
auf den Beinen ist
«In allem folgt diese Aktion
dem Gedankengut
der Cyber-Hippies
aus den Siebzigern»
sagt er
«Nämlich
dass der menschliche Körper
bloss noch
ein störendes Element ist
der Körper

will schlafen
und essen
und schlecht gelaunt sein
aber ich will
eigentlich
nur Informationen verarbeiten
und zwar ohne Pause
ohne Schlaf
ich will eine einzige
Informationsverarbeitungsmaschine sein
gleichzeitig
auch das folgt diesem Gedanken
intervenieren wir künstlerisch
in Bahrain
ohne vor Ort zu sein
ohne also
den eigenen Körper
in Gefahr zu bringen»

Dann
die Prognosen
dass das Paket sein Ziel erreicht
hatten schlecht gestanden
weil Nabeel Rajab
in einem Gefängnis sitzt
weil Pakete
mit elektronischen Geräten
die Signale senden
es sowieso schwierig haben
Sicherheitskontrollen zu passieren
dann also
am Zoll des Flughafens in Dubai
am Samstagmorgen
8:55 Londoner Zeit
und 12:55 Dubai-Zeit
nach fünf Tagen Reise
einfach so
ohne Vorwarnung
ohne Erklärung

17.01.2013 19:06 — Julian Assange.

«Wir wissen nicht
was passiert ist»
behauptete Fedex später
ohne es nach Bahrain geschafft zu haben
zu Nabeel Rajab
im Gefängnis sitzend
für Kritik am Königshaus
und ohne das Bild
eines Sicherheitsbeamten
der das Paket aufreisst
und in die Kamera starrt
erlosch
von der einen Sekunde
auf die andere
das GPS-Signal des Pakets
von Julian Assange
für Nabeel Rajab

Dubai, 25. November 2013: An einem Freitag im November flogen Adnan und Doma, von London und Zürich kommend, nach Dubai. Für einen zweiten Versuch. Sie wollten das Paket für Nabeel Rajab in Dubai aufgeben, den nächsten Flieger nehmen und sobald sie in der Luft wären, würde Carmen von Zürich aus die Übertragung starten. «Ich war ein wenig nervös mit all den elektronischen Geräten im Koffer, aber wir kamen problemlos durch den Zoll», sagte Doma ein paar Wochen später, als man sich mit Assange zu Raclette und Weisswein traf, um ein Fazit zu ziehen.

Carmen hatte den Käse wieder aus der Schweiz mitgebracht, zwei Kilogramm, und Silberzwiebeln, Speck, Weisswein und einen Raclette-Ofen, der von der Botschaftssicherheit akzeptiert und nicht abgewiesen wurde als «elektronisches Gerät».

«Die ganze Stadt», sagte Doma, «wirkte ein wenig wie ein grosser Flughafen. Wolkenkratzer, Kameras, keine Menschen auf den Strassen – Überwachungsarchitektur. In der Metro ist es sehr, sehr still. Man getraut sich kaum zu reden. Dubai wirkte auf mich wie eine Stadt der lebenden Toten, und alle zehn Meter ein Foto des Scheichs.»

«Die Zukunft», sagte Assange.

Doma und Adnan hatten sich für zwei Tage in einem Hotel einquartiert. Sie versuchten, im Meer zu schwimmen, aber der Zugang zum Meer war allerorts privatisiert und kostete 75 Dollar. Auf dem Flughafen entdeckten sie ein riesiges Fedex-Gebäude. «Beim Abgleich der GPS-Daten stellte sich heraus», sagte Doma, «dass dort in jenem Fedex-Gebäude der Kontakt zum ersten Paket verloren gegangen war.» Man gab das neue Paket in einer Poststelle auf, stieg ins nächste Flugzeug. Dann startete Carmen die Übertragung.

«#postdrone ist wieder online. Wir starten einen zweiten Versuch. Ein Paket für Herrn Rajab. http://rajab.bitnik.org/live.html #postdrone @wikileaks @NABEELRAJAB»

Zwanzig Stunden später, kaum hatte das Paket den Cargobereich des Flughafens erreicht, verschwand das Signal wieder, und Carmen twitterte: «Der Flughafen von Dubai scheint kein guter Ort zu sein für unsere Postdrohnen. Seit 48 Stunden fehlt vom zweiten Paket für @nabeelrajab jegliches Lebenszeichen.» Und später: «Dubai, die grosse Firewall nach Bahrain. Noch immer keine Neuigkeiten, was das zweite Paket für @nabeelrajab angeht. Es verschwand vor drei Wochen am Zoll von Dubai.»

17.01.2013 19:08 — Innenansicht, Botschaft Ecuadors, London.

1. Auflage 27. Februar 2014
Copyright © 2014 Echtzeit Verlag GmbH, Basel
Alle Rechte vorbehalten

ISBN 978-3-905800-81-4

Unterstützt von: Helmhaus Zürich, Stadt Zürich Kultur

Tweets, Bilder und Text:
Copyleft 2014 !Mediengruppe Bitnik, all rights reversed
http://wwwwwwwwwwwwwwwwwwww.bitnik.org/assange/
http://rajab.bitnik.org/

Autor: Daniel Ryser, !Mediengruppe Bitnik
Lektorat: Armin Büttner
Korrektorat: Birgit Althaler
Gestaltung: Müller+Hess, Basel
Druck: Ebner & Spiegel, Ulm

www.echtzeit.ch

17.01.2013 19:09 — Hallo Dunkelheit, alter Freund.
17.01.2013 19:31 — Das war eine Live-Mailart-Performance der !Mediengruppe Bitnik featuring Julian Assange.
17.01.2013 19:37 — Danke und gute Nacht!